Sustainable User Experience

From Practice to Integration–A Guide for UX Professionals and Business Leaders

Monika Schirmeier

This publication is the Englisch translation of the original German edition authored by Monika Schirmeier and published by Haufe. Original title: *Nachhaltige User Experience. Ein Handbuch für die praktische Umsetzung und erfolgreiche Unternehmensintegration*. The English edition was translated by the author.

ISBN (Book): 978-80-11-06879-0
ISBN (PDF): 978-80-11-06880-6
ISBN (ePub): 978-80-11-07072-4

The Amazon Endure typeface was designed by 2K/DENMARK in 2025.

Use of inclusive language
This book uses gender-neutral and inclusive language throughout. All individuals are addressed equally and respectfully, regardless of gender or identity.

Geographical Frame
This book takes a European perspective. Legal, cultural, or institutional references reflect this background. However, the broader concepts and discussions are globally relevant and applicable.

DEDICATION

This book is dedicated to my son, Nico. He is part of a new generation that inspires hope and carries the potential to make our world a better place.

KNOWLEDGE IS POWER.

CONTENTS

ACKNOWLEDGMENTS

I would like to thank Professors Nora Bilz and Steffi Neukirchen. Their encouragement to embark on this book project, along with their support and motivation, laid the foundation for this work.

I am also deeply grateful to my husband. After I decided to write this book, he would often say with a wink that it could be done "on the side"—and in doing so, gave me the gentle push I needed to pull through. His confidence in me, along with his patience throughout this journey, has been invaluable.

FOREWORD

For several years, I volunteered alongside my work as a UX/UI designer. I supported children, young people, and individuals who arrived in Germany from other countries and needed help to adjust to their new environment. More recently, I spent time abroad—first contributing to a project in Israel that offers emotional and technical support to Holocaust survivors, and later working with an organisation in Scotland that supports homeless people.

Working with older adults, however, has always held a special place in my heart. For over a decade, my team and I regularly organised events for older adults in my hometown. Later, I turned this passion into a profession. For over two years, I travelled across Germany, helping older adults access and use digital media. I saw firsthand how difficult it is for them to develop digital skills—and how discouraging it is when confusing navigation stands in their way.

This experience gradually shifted my focus toward accessible design. As I became more involved in digital accessibility, I realised how essential it is for shaping truly inclusive products. When we design with people of all ages, abilities, and physical conditions in mind, we foster inclusion—and give companies a real competitive advantage by reaching wider audiences and creating greater impact.

The growing integration of accessibility into digital product design—backed by legal standards in many countries— is a meaningful move toward more inclusive design. It is also encouraging to see a growing trend toward prioritising user needs over purely corporate goals. But in focusing solely on people, we risk overlooking another crucial part of the picture: *our environment.*

We live in a deeply interconnected world, where balance depends on how well systems work together. That is why I felt the need to broaden my perspective and consciously integrate environmental sustainability into my design practice. At first, UX had few references or standards for sustainable design. But that is changing. Today, more professionals recognise that a holistic approach—one that considers both people and the planet—leads to better user experiences and to long-term responsibility and success.

This approach calls for a shift in mindset. It asks us to challenge traditional thinking and place greater importance on lasting values over short-term gain.

Sustainability is now a key issue for society. This presents a significant challenge for companies, as they face growing pressure to embed sustainable practices across all areas of their operations. I use the word "challenge" deliberately—because although the concept is not new, it remains difficult to implement. Too often, sustainability is treated as a trendy "nice to have," rather than a strategic foundation.

That is why I wrote this book. It brings together research, practical experience, cross-industry insights, and interviews. It is for designers, product managers, executives, stakeholders, and anyone involved in shaping digital experiences. Real impact happens when everyone in the process understands the value of sustainable design and works together to make it happen.

I wish you many inspiring and enriching moments with this book!

Monika

INTRODUCTION

Around 60 percent of the global population has access to the internet. People spend a considerable part of their waking lives online—according to estimates, over *40 percent*. This equates to around six to seven hours per day spent consuming digital content, communicating, or otherwise interacting with digital interfaces.

In a world where our daily actions have an ever-increasing impact on the environment, it has become essential to consider sustainability in all areas of our lives—from our consumer behaviour to the products and services we use. It is time to become more conscious of our choices and their impact on the planet.

In the digital age, delivering a positive user experience is crucial. Companies, face the challenge of offering products and services that meet the needs of their target audience while aligning with the principles of sustainability. Designers, take on the task of translating business requirements into creative solutions, thereby sharing ecological responsibility.

This book explores how sustainability and user experience intersect to support responsible design decisions and drive ecologically, socially, and economically sustainable outcomes for both companies and society. It also shows how usability, user-centered design, and life-centered design can directly support sustainable design.

The book places special emphasis on the role of sustainability for designers and companies. It explores how sustainable user experiences appeal to target audiences and help raise awareness of sustainable behaviour. With concrete design and management approaches—and a look at future developments such as the use of artificial intelligence—this book offers a comprehensive foundation for anyone seeking to shape creating digital products with responsibility and a long-term perspective.

1. SUSTAINABILITY–A HISTORICAL OVERVIEW

Current global and planetary events highlight the importance of using available resources. Over the years, significant steps to protect the environment, promote social justice, and ensure economic stability have been taken by various actors. These milestones have helped make sustainability a central theme in various areas of life. While implementation and integration are not yet complete, these milestones have laid a solid foundation for further progress.

1.1 Milestones on the Road to Sustainability

The global focus on sustainability began with the 1972 United Nations Conference on the Human Environment in Stockholm and the report *Limits to Growth*, which first acknowledged the tensions between environmental limits and economic development[1]. The *World Conservation Strategy of the International Union for the Conservation of Nature* (IUCN) followed in the 1980s. It promoted the integration of nature conservation and sustainable development, aiming to preserve ecological processes, maintain genetic diversity, and ensure the sustainable use of species and ecosystems.[2]

The Brundtland Report

In 1982, the United Nations General Assembly established the World Commission on Environment and Development. Its 1987 report, *Our Common Future*, addressed urgent global environmental challenges and their link to economic development. It emphasised the need for a long-term, integrative perspective that unites ecological sustainability, economic growth, and social justice.

The Brundtland Report called for a shift in political, economic, and societal thinking to safeguard ecological, social, and economic foundations for future generations. It defined sustainability as a global and holistic principle and introduced its now-famous definition:

[1] Meadows, Meadows, Randers, & Behrens, 1972.
[2] IUCN, 1980.

> *"Development that meets the needs of the present without compromising the ability of future generations to meet their own need."*
>
> (Brundtland 1987, S. 54)

The report laid the groundwork for major global environmental initiatives and raised awareness of the need for a long-term outlook and a shared global responsibility for a sustainable future.

Earth Summit and Agenda 21

The 1992 United Nations Conference on Environment and Development (UNCED) in Rio de Janeiro[3] marked another key milestone in global sustainability efforts. This summit resulted in *Agenda 21*[4], a detailed action plan, and international agreements on climate change, biodiversity, and the principles for forestry. The key goals of Agenda 21 include:

- **Addressing environmental challenges**: Urgent environmental issues, including climate change, deforestation, land degradation, and water scarcity, require immediate attention.
- **Promoting sustainable development**: The effort focuses on balancing economic, social, and environmental priorities.
- **Building partnerships**: Collaboration among governments, international organisations, civil society, and the private sector is essential to achieving the Sustainable Development Goals.

Millenium Development Goals (MDGs)

At the 2000 United Nations Millennium Summit, 147 countries agreed on the Millennium Development Goals (MDGs)[5], which addressed key aspects of poverty—including hunger, disease, exclusion, and inadequate housing—while also targeting education, gender equality, and environmental issues.

Goal 7—ensuring environmental sustainability—encouraged measures to conserve natural resources, halt deforestation, and improve access to clean water and sanitation. These efforts laid the groundwork for the more comprehensive and long-term Sustainable Development Goals (SDGs).

Agenda 2030 and the SDGs (2015)

In 2015, the United Nations adopted the 2030 Agenda for Sustainable Development, which established 17 interconnected SDGs and 169 associated targets[6]. These goals address a wide spectrum of global challenges—from basic needs such as education, health, poverty eradication, and environmental protection. The 2030 Agenda also recognises the transformative potential of global connectivity and knowledge-based societies. It emphasises that the

---

[3] United Nations, 1993.
[4] Agenda 21, 1992.
[5] United Nations, 2000.
[6] United Nations, 2015.

SDGs must be dynamic and adaptable to respond to unpredictable global developments—particularly considering rapid digitalisation and the rise of the internet, including social media.

Importantly, the SDGs offer a vision for a more equitable and sustainable world and also a concrete roadmap for achieving it. SDGs provide governments, organisations, and individuals with a shared framework for long-term impact—grounded in cooperation, innovation, and resilience.

Germany has committed both to the domestic implementation of the SDGs and to supporting their global realisation. In 2021, the German Federal Government updated its national sustainability strategy in alignment with the 2030 Agenda.[7]

The SDGs include the following sustainability goals[8]:

1. **No poverty**: End poverty in all its forms everywhere.
2. **Zero hunger**: End hunger, achieve food security and improved nutrition and promote sustainable agriculture.
3. **Good health and wellbeing**: Ensure healthy lives and promote well-being for all at all ages.
4. **Quality education**: Ensure inclusive and equitable quality education and promote lifelong learning opportunities for all.
5. **Gender equality**: Achieve gender equality and empower all women and girls.
6. **Clean water and sanitation**: Ensure availability and sustainable management of water and sanitation for all.
7. **Affordable and clean energy**: Ensure access to affordable, reliable, sustainable and modern energy for all.
8. **Decent work and economic growth**: Promote sustained, inclusive and sustainable economic growth, full and productive employment and decent work for all.
9. **Industry, innovation, and infrastructure**: Build resilient infrastructure, promote inclusive and sustainable industrialisation and foster innovation.
10. **Reduced inequalities**: Reduce inequality within and among countries.
11. **Sustainable cities and communities**: Make cities and human settlements inclusive, safe, resilient and sustainable.
12. **Responsible consumption and production**: Ensure sustainable consumption and production patterns.
13. **Climate action**: Take urgent action to combat climate change and its impacts.
14. **Life below water**: Conserve and sustainably use the oceans, seas and marine resources for sustainable development.
15. **Life on land**: Protect, restore and promote sustainable use of terrestrial

[7] Bundesregierung, 2021.

[8] United Nations, 2015.

ecosystems, sustainably manage forests, combat desertification, and halt and reverse land degradation and halt biodiversity loss.
16. **Peace, justice and strong institutions**: Promote peaceful and inclusive societies for sustainable development, provide access to justice for all, and build effective, accountable and inclusive institutions at all levels.
17. **Partnerships for the goals**: Strengthen the means of implementation and revitalise the Global Partnership for Sustainable Development.

Conclusion

These milestones have laid the groundwork for a global understanding that using resources responsibly, promoting social justice, and maintaining economic stability are essential. Today, these principles shape political, economic, and technological decisions worldwide and guide efforts to shape a sustainable future.

1.2 Strategic Shifts in Companies

In the 1990s and early 2000s, sustainability emerged primarily through the lens of Corporate Social Responsibility (CSR). A seminal contribution from this period was John Elkington's book *Cannibals with Forks*[9] in which he introduced the concept of the *"Triple Bottom Line"*—commonly referred to as the "three Ps": *People*, *Planet*, and *Profit*. This model expanded the traditional profit-oriented perspective to include environmental and social dimensions, urging companies to embed sustainability as a long-term guiding principle.

Circular Economy and Zero Waste

In parallel, new approaches, such as the circular economy and the zero-waste movement emerged. The circular economy advocates for a transition from traditional linear economic models ("take, make, dispose") toward closed-loop systems that aim to minimise waste and use resources as efficiently as possible.[10] Similarly, the zero-waste movement encourages both businesses and individuals to reduce waste to a minimum and adopt practices that maximise resource recovery.[11] These models support CSR by providing concrete strategies for resource conservation and environmental impact reduction.

ESG Criteria: A New Benchmark for Sustainability

The term ESG—Environmental, Social, and Governance—emerged to meet the growing need for measuring and comparing sustainability performance. First introduced in 2004 by the UN report *Who Cares Wins*, initiated by Kofi Annan, ESG criteria aimed to integrate sustainability into financial markets.[12] In 2006, the launch of the UN Principles for Responsible Investment (UN PRI) further

---

[9] Ecklington, 1998.
[10] Stumpf & Prof. Dr. Baumgartner, 2022.
[11] Zero Waste International Alliance, 2025.
[12] The Global Compact, 2004.

encouraged investors to consider ESG factors in decision-making.[13] Three key dimensions shape the ESG framework:

- **Environmental**: A company's ecological impact, including climate change, pollution, resource use, and biodiversity.
- **Social**: The company's relationship with its stakeholders, including labor practices, diversity, human rights, and community engagement.
- **Governance**: Internal systems of control, transparency, business ethics, and regulatory compliance.

ESG Rating and reporting

The ESG concept includes two key mechanisms: *ESG reporting* and *ESG ratings*. These tools help companies improve and communicate their sustainability performance. Specialised agencies develop ESG ratings, and financial institutions and rating organisations use them to assess companies and guide investment and financing decisions. Simultaneously, companies prepare and publish their own ESG reports to inform stakeholders and the public about their environmental, social, and governance efforts.

ESG Ratings

ESG ratings are typically based on data, indicators, and rating systems that allow a company's sustainability performance to be quantified and compared. Rating agencies generally rate companies on a scale and classify them into ESG indices or rankings.[14]

ESG Reporting

ESG reporting refers to the disclosure of sustainability-related information by companies themselves. This means that companies publish reports that outline their environmental, social, and governance performance to inform stakeholders about their sustainability efforts.[15]

An ESG rating extends beyond traditional financial metrics and evaluates a broad range of company activities, such as waste management, energy efficiency, employee well-being, social engagement, and the responsible use of resources. This marks progress toward a more comprehensive sustainability assessment.

Challenges in Standardisation

Despite their value, ESG assessments face challenges due to the lack of consistent standards. For instance, a company in a high-emission industry

[13] UNEP Finance Initiative; UN Global Compact, 2006.
[14] OECD, 2025.
[15] OECD, 2025.

might still receive a favourable ESG rating within its sector, despite its broader environmental impact. This raises concerns about the credibility and comparability of such assessments.[16]

The Role of the European Securities and Markets Authority (ESMA)

Established in 2011, the European Securities and Markets Authority oversees financial market regulation and monitors ESG disclosures. One of its goals is to prevent greenwashing—the practice of presenting a product, service, or company as more environmentally friendly than it is.[17] ESMA aims to prevent greenwashing by developing clear criteria for evaluating ESG products and supervising rating agencies. This enhances trust in sustainability claims and protects stakeholders from misleading practices.

Greenwashing: a Persistent Risk

Environmental activist Jay Westervelt coined the term "greenwashing" in 1986, criticising superficial sustainability claims in the hospitality industry. In his essay, he exposed how hotels often used towel reuse appeals as marketing tactics to mask environmentally harmful business practices.[18]

The Oxford English Dictionary formally recognised greenwashing in 1999, and it remains a concern today. It refers to deceptive practices, where companies exaggerate or fabricate their environmental efforts for reputational or financial gain.

Conclusion

The evolution of corporate sustainability strategy has passed several important milestones—from the Triple Bottom Line to ESG criteria, circular economy models, and regulatory oversight by ESMA. Despite ongoing challenges, these frameworks provide a strong basis for embedding sustainability into business practices and driving long-term, responsible growth.

1.3 Sustainability in Digital Experiences

Integrating sustainability into user experience is an ongoing process, without a clear starting point. Over the years, various movements and approaches have emerged and significantly influenced how sustainability principles are applied to the design and development of digital products.

The 2010s: Focus on Target Groups and Sustainability

In the 2010s, methodologies such as design thinking and human-centered design (HCD) placed an increasing emphasis on users' needs and experiences.

---

[16] Johnson, 2023; Laker, 2023.
[17] ESMA, 2023.
[18] Becker-Olsen & Potucek, 2013.

Initially aimed at improving usability, these approaches began to integrate sustainability as an essential value.

Influential publications like *Design is the Problem* by N. Shedroff[19], *Change by Design* by T. Brown[20], and *The Design of Everyday Things* by D. Norman[21] helped solidify this shift. At the same time, the understanding of sustainable user experience expanded to include social responsibility, reflected in accessible, inclusive, and design for longevity.

Sustainable Web Manifesto[22]

Initiated by Tom Greenwood, Tim Frick, Mike Gifford and other members of the sustainable web community, the Sustainable Web Manifesto is a public commitment calling for a more sustainable internet, built on six key principles:

- **Clean:** Services should be powered by renewable energy
- **Efficient:** Digital products should consume minimal energy and resources
- **Open:** Promote open access to information and empower users with control over their data.
- **Honest:** Design and content should be free from manipulation and exploitation
- **Regenerative**: Products should actively support people and the planet
- **Resilient**: Services should remain functional wherever and whenever they are most needed

Web Sustainability Guidelines (WSG 1.0)

Integrated into W3C Standards in 2024, the WSG offers a methodological framework for embedding sustainability into the entire lifecycle of digital products—from design and development to business models.[23] Key principles:

- Efficiency and resource conservation
- Accessibility and inclusion
- Durability and reusability
- Transparency and awareness

These guidelines support using an interdisciplinary approach from the earliest stages of a project. They encourage designers and developers to address sustainability concerns proactively rather than retrofitting them later. WSG also supports sustainable business models that focuses long-term value over short-term profits.

Conclusion

Together, the Sustainable Web Manifesto and the Web Sustainability Guidelines have laid a solid foundation for integrating sustainability into

[19] Shedroff, 2009.
[20] Brown, 2019.
[21] Norman, 2013.
[22] https://www.sustainablewebmanifesto.com
[23] W3C, 2024.

digital experiences. They mark an important step toward a future where user experience is functional and enjoyable and also responsible and regenerative. With continuously evolving tools, standards, and technologies, designers now have the opportunity and responsibility to transform sustainable UX from a guiding principle into a global norm.

1.4 Summary and Conclusion

Sustainability has evolved into a global guiding principle, shaped by milestones like the Brundtland Report, Agenda 21, and the Sustainable Development Goals. Businesses increasingly adopt frameworks like the triple bottom line, circular economy, and ESG to align with sustainability.

In the digital world, the Sustainable Web Manifesto and the Web Sustainability Guidelines support resource-efficient and inclusive solutions. These developments form the foundation for a sustainable future in business, politics, and technology.

2 HOW DO USER EXPERIENCE AND SUSTAINABILITY FIT TOGETHER?

User experience and usability are fundamental to human-centered design. While usability focuses on effectiveness, efficiency, and satisfaction during use, user experience expands this approach to include the holistic perception and emotional connection of users throughout the entire interaction cycle.

Both concepts make digital and physical interactions intuitive, accessible, and enjoyable – consistently aligned with the needs of the target audience. However, when the design of digital applications shifts its focus beyond the user's needs to include the wider ecosystem, new opportunities arise to reduce negative ecological and social impacts. This marks a paradigm shift: from user-centered approaches to sustainable UX, which considers the environmental, societal, and economic consequences throughout the design process.

The following section will first examine the fundamentals of usability and user-centered design, to establish a solid foundation for further discussion and to better understand development approaches aimed at sustainability.

2.1 Usability: Effective, Efficient, and Satisfying

Usability refers to how effectively, efficiently, and satisfactorily a product supports the user in achieving their goals in a defined context of use. DIN EN ISO 9241-11 defines usability as:

> *"...extent to which a system, product or service can be used by specified users to achieve specified goals with effectiveness, efficiency and satisfaction in a specified context of use."*
>
> (ISO - International Organization for Standardization, 2018, section 3.1.1)

- Effectiveness means users complete their tasks accurately and fully.
- Efficiency refers to achieving goals with minimal time and effort – optimising mental load and interactions.
- Satisfaction shows a positive user experience through intuitive handling, ease of use, and fulfilment of expectations.

2.2 UX and User-Centered Design: Focusing on People

User-centered design emerged in the 1940s in aviation and engineering, later extending to Human-Computer Interaction (HCI) in the 1960s and 70s. Ethnographic methods like contextual interviews and shadowing added depth by incorporating user perspectives into the design process.[24]

User-centered design and user experience are defined in ISO 9241-210:

- **User-centered design** User-centered design is a *process* that ensures systems are both useful and usable by focusing on users' needs and incorporating their perspectives throughout every stage of development.
- **User experience** is the *outcome* of this process and is defined as a person's perceptions and responses resulting from the actual and/or expected use of a product, system, or service.

Designing successful solutions requires a deep understanding of the target audience. By focusing on their needs, desires, and challenges, it is possible to create products that are functional and emotionally engaging.

The human-centered approach has fundamentally transformed the way teams design digital solutions. In the past, developers often prioritised functional and economic goals. Today, successful product design requires a comprehensive understanding of the user, including ease of use, usage context, and personal relevance.

2.3 Life-Centered Design: Thinking Holistically

The shift from conventional UX to sustainable UX represents a major evolution in design philosophy. Sustainable UX broadens the focus beyond users' needs to include sustainability and social responsibility. This paradigm, often referred to as *Life-Centered Design*, considers ecological, social and economic responsibility as essential components of the design process.

It turns UX into a tool for designing a more sustainable world. The terms Sustainable UX, Environment-Centered Design, Humanity-Centered Design, or Society-Centered Design often describe this broader approach.

ISO 9241-210's section 8 urges designers to consider the ecological, social, and economic effects of their work as part of socially responsible and sustainable design. It explicitly calls on them to reflect on how their solutions will affect not just users, but also the planet and systems of governance now and into future.

By considering long-term consequences for both people and the environment, life-centered design:

- Increases usability and accessibility
- Reduces stress, discomfort, and frustration
- Improves positive user experience
- Contributes to sustainability goals

[24] Pratt & Nunes, 2012.

- Sharpens brand identity and competitiveness

Systems thinking and sustainability

In *Design is the Problem* from Nathan Shedroff[25], he emphasises the deep connection between human needs and the surrounding systems, be it the environment or the social structures in which we live. The environment, society, and cultural values are part of a larger system whose components are in constant interaction. It also clarifies that sustainability not only aims meeting the needs of the present, but also ensuring the long-term stability of the entire system. Prioritising human needs requires equal attention to the broader system they are part of, as the two are inherently connected. He writes:

> *"The essence of this definition [of sustainability], which may not be obvious immediately, is that needs are not just human, they're systemic. Even if you only care about humans, in order to care for humans, you need to take care of the system – (the environment) that you live in. And this environment does not include just the closed system we call the planet Earth. It also includes the human systems we live in – our societies – and the forming, changing, and constantly evolving values, ethics, religion, and culture that encompass these societies. We are not separable from each other, and we can't ignore the effects of the whole – nor should we."*
>
> (Shedroff, 2009, S. 33–34)

Sustainability requires acknowledging our interdependence with environmental and social systems. Similarly, Patagonia's founder Yvon Chouinard states:[26]

> *"There's no such thing as sustainability—only levels of it. It is a process, not a goal."*
> (Yvon Chouinard, in an interview with Little)

And Don Norman, professor and co-founder of the Nielsen Norman Group, defines sustainability as the ability to maintain something over a long period of time or even permanently.[27]

2.4 Conclusion

User-centered design has evolved into life-centered thinking. By expanding the focus from immediate user satisfaction to the long-term impact on the environment and society, UX becomes a vehicle for sustainability.

This approach, now supported by standards like ISO 9241-210, enables creating products that are user-friendly and resource-efficient, socially responsible, and future-ready.

---

[25] Shedroff, 2019.
[26] Little, 2004.
[27] Norman, 2023.

3 WHY SUSTAINABILITY IS ESSENTIAL FOR COMPANIES AND SOCIETY

People often underestimate the ecological footprint of the digital sector. The CO_2 emissions from smart devices, the internet itself, and the supporting infrastructure already account for about 4 percent of global greenhouse gas emissions. At first glance, this may not seem like much, but even with current usage levels, it already surpasses the emissions of the much-debated aviation industry.[28]

One of the main reasons for this is the ongoing process of digitalisation, which is accompanied by a sharp increase in the volume of data that needs to be processed and stored. Digital usage is steadily rising, and the demand for powerful data centers and networks continues to grow.[29]

Video streaming, the use of cloud services, and the rapid spread of connected devices—such as smart homes and the Internet of Things (IoT)—are major contributors to this trend.[30] On top of that, technological advancements like artificial intelligence (AI) and machine learning (ML) require massive computational power, which further drives up energy consumption.

The rising energy demand for digital infrastructure and its associated CO_2 emissions clearly shows an urgent need for more sustainable solutions. Without significant progress in designing more environmentally friendly technologies and promoting responsible digital usage, the digital sector's ecological footprint will increase substantially.

Driving Change With UX

Designing a sustainable user experience holds the potential to reduce the resource consumption of digital products through intentional design decisions. Efficiency and effectiveness are key: quickly and directly achieving user goals in digital applications reduces server requests, thus minimising overall data processing.

While reducing resource consumption is important, sustainable design involves much more. Equally important are broader goals, such as promoting

[28] Hazas, 2023; Marks, 2022.

[29] Hintemann, 2017; Marks, 2022.

[30] Hintemann & Hinterholzer, 2020.

social equity, supporting economic resilience, and protecting the environment and biodiversity. In addition, sustainable UX encourages a circular economy and focuses on creating durable, resource-efficient, and sustainable products.

3.1 Society in Transition: Sustainability Affects us All

Germany ranks among the ten countries with the highest carbon dioxide (CO_2) emissions worldwide. China tops the list, accounting for just over 30 percent of global CO_2 emissions.[31]

What is CO_2?

Carbon dioxide (CO_2) is a colourless, odourless gas composed of one carbon and two oxygen atoms. While it occurs naturally in respiration and decomposition, human activities—such as the burning of fossil fuels and deforestation—have drastically increased its concentration in the atmosphere.

CO_2 is a primary driver of global warming, as it traps heat, intensifying the greenhouse effect.

Global Climate Action

Higher CO_2 levels have many serious environmental consequences. CO_2 is one of the key factors in global warming because CO_2 traps heat in the Earth's atmosphere, creating a kind of greenhouse effect. Human activities, such as burning fossil fuels (oil, coal, natural gas), deforestation, and industrial processes, release more CO_2 into the atmosphere, increasing the greenhouse effect. This increased greenhouse effect means that more heat remains on the Earth, global temperatures rise, which we refer to as global warming.

According to the IPCC's (Intergovernmental Panel on Climate Change) first climate report (1990)[32], the global temperature had already increased by 0.3 to 0.6°C compared to pre-industrial levels[33]. Today, the average has reached +1.1°C, with acceleration since the 1970s. Since 1970, surface temperatures have increased more rapidly than during any 50-year period in the past two millennia.

The 2015 Paris Agreement seeks to limit global warming to well below 2°C, preferably 1.5°C[34], a crucial target for vulnerable nations such as Barbados, Fiji, and the Maldives, where even small temperature increases could have devastating effects.[35] By 2050, over a billion people may live in low-lying areas at risk from rising sea-level.

---

[31] Global Carbon Project, 2023.
[32] IPCC, 1992.
[33] This refers to the years between 1850 and 1900.
[34] BMUV, 2015.
[35] UN Climate Change, 2021.

What is the Paris Agreement?

The Paris Agreement, officially known as the United Nations Framework Convention on Climate Change (UNFCCC), is an international agreement based on the 21st Conference of the Parties (COP21), adopted in Paris in December 2015. It is a historic multilateral agreement that aims to limit the global temperature rise, combat climate change and promote global adaptation to the effects of climate change.

Recommended actions to lower emissions:

- Transition to renewable energy (decarbonisation)
- Extend the lifecycle of digital and physical products
- Promote responsible digital consumption

Giving up the internet is not an option—but using it responsibly is.

Climate and Agriculture

Climate change has profound effects on global agriculture and food systems. Rising temperatures, shifting weather patterns, and extreme weather events, like floods, droughts, and heatwaves, are making cultivation conditions increasingly unpredictable and difficult.

Two key factors are critical:

- **Drought at the wrong time:** Crops need water at specific growth phases. A dry spell during flowering or fruit setting can drastically reduce yields.
- **Rain at the wrong time:** Unseasonal or excessive rainfall can destroy harvests, lead to fungal diseases, or erode fertile soil.

Agronomist Wilfried Bommert, an agronomist, and spokesperson for the World Food Institute in Berlin, warns in an interview that a global temperature increase of 2°C could lead to substantial yield losses or even complete crop failures in some regions.[36] The faster the rise, the less time ecosystems have to adapt. Even in temperate regions like Central Europe, new pests are spreading due to warmer winters. The cherry vinegar fly, for example, is now damaging fruit crops such as cherries and grapes, which were previously unaffected.

This shows that the threat is twofold: not only do plants struggle under new climate conditions, but rising temperatures also favour the spread of pests and plant diseases into regions previously unaffected.

In the long term, this jeopardises global food security—not just through lower yields, but through reduced biodiversity, economic losses in agriculture, and increasing prices for consumers.

[36] Bommert, 2017.

Ocean Acidification and Climate Feedback Loops

The ocean and the cryosphere (the frozen parts of the earth, such as glaciers and ice sheets) are crucial components of the global climate system. Oceans, covering about 70 percent of earth, control and regulate temperature, absorb CO_2, and maintain biodiversity.[37] The cryosphere reflects sunlight and stabilises sea levels. Together, these systems act as climate regulators, but they are under severe stress because of human-caused emissions.

One of the ocean's most critical roles is as a carbon sink: it absorbs about a quarter of CO_2 emitted by human activity. While this process slows global warming, it leads to a serious side effect - *ocean acidification.*[38]

When CO_2 dissolves in seawater, it reacts to form carbonic acid, which increases the concentration of hydrogen ions (H^+) in the water. This *lowers the pH*, making the ocean more acidic. Even small changes in this shift dramatically impact marine ecosystems.

- **Coral reefs**, which rely on calcium carbonate to build their skeletons, become more fragile and struggle to grow.
- **Shellfish and crustaceans** find it harder to form and maintain their shells.
- **Food chains** are disrupted as planktonic organisms—some of which also rely on calcium carbonate—decline in number.

Beyond acidification, the warming of the oceans leads to reduced oxygen levels, particularly in deep waters. This creates "*dead zones,*" where marine life cannot survive. Rising sea temperatures also change current patterns, affect weather systems, and increase the intensity of storms.

The cryosphere is likewise destabilising. Melting glaciers and polar ice sheets contribute to sea level rise and reduce Earth's albedo (its ability to reflect sunlight). Less reflection means more heat absorption, which speeds up warming—a climate feedback loop. Permafrost thawing in the Arctic could release vast amounts of methane—a potent greenhouse gas—into the atmosphere, creating another dangerous self-reinforcing effect.

Protecting the oceans is therefore not just about marine life—it is about the stability of the entire planet.

Conclusion: A Shared Responsibility

The impact of climate change is wide-reaching, deeply interconnected, and increasingly urgent. Rising temperatures, shifting weather patterns, ocean acidification, biodiversity loss, and threats to food and water security problems—these factors create a complex web of global risk. These developments endanger ecosystems and the social and economic stability of human societies.

---

[37] IPCC, 2019.
[38] IPCC, 2019.

What has become clear is that sustainability is no longer a niche concern—it affects everyone. From farmers in drought-stricken regions to families in coastal cities at risk of flooding, from supply chains reliant on stable climates to healthcare systems facing new disease patterns, the consequences of inaction are already visible.

Awareness is increasing concurrently. International agreements such as the Paris Agreement provide political frameworks, but real change depends on what individuals, organisations, and businesses do—every day. It is a shared responsibility.

Digitalisation plays a key role in both the problem and the solution. Although the digital industry is a significant contributor to emissions and energy consumption, its potential for promoting sustainability through smart design, enhancing efficiency, and raising awareness is immense. UX designers, developers, and decision-makers in tech are in a unique position to influence positive change—through conscious design, efficient systems, transparent communication, and accessibility.

True sustainability requires a systemic approach that considers social, ecological, and economic factors together. It requires rethinking, not what we consume, but how we design, communicate, and operate. In this context, digital sustainability is not a contradiction—but a crucial foundation for a livable future.

3.2 Business Responsibility for the Planet

Contemporary society is characterised by overconsumption, short product life cycles, and a culture of convenience. This pattern reflects a broader systemic trend shaped by how many companies operate—prioritising low-cost, fast-to-market products that are difficult to repair or reuse. Systemic change requires more than individual consumer action. Companies play a central role in influencing consumption habits and determining the sustainability of the products and services they offer.

Many organisations still encourage harmful practices—by promoting excessive use, designing short-lived products, or withholding information about environmental impact. From physical goods to digital services, teams need to apply the same logic consistently across the entire life cycle.

Physical Products: Convenience at a Cost

Paper cups are a telling example. Germans alone use about 2.8 billion paper cups annually.[39] Typically, manufactures coat these cups with plastic to prevent leaks, despite their perceived recyclability. This composite design makes recycling difficult and costly. A common practice is burning these cups, which increases CO_2 and disrupts the circular flow of materials.

---

[39] Suhr, 2019.

Digital devices follow a similar pattern. Smartphones, tablets, and laptops contain valuable raw materials like gold, copper, and rare earth elements. Mining companies extract these materials under environmentally and often socially questionable conditions. Planned obsolescence is a design feature in many devices; making repairs difficult, updates incompatible, and replacements more attractive than maintenance. As a result, e-waste is one of the fastest-growing waste streams worldwide.

Digital Products: Invisible Waste

The same problems show up in the digital world—just less visibly. Here, waste takes the form of data and energy:

- **Lacking a clear focus on target audiences:** designs appeal to everyone instead of meeting the needs of a defined core audience.
- **Visual overload**: excessive use of images, videos, and animations, distracts from essential content and increases energy consumption.
- **Company interests over user needs:** ads and product placements often outweigh personalised, user-centered content.
- **Non-optimised file sizes** (e.g. high-resolution images and videos) increase energy use unnecessarily.
- **Unfocused content** leads to longer user journeys, more server requests, and higher bandwidth needs.
- **Dark patterns**: design choices that manipulate users into behaviours they would not consciously choose. Dark patterns focus on short-term gains over user trust or environmental impact.

Often, companies choose to flood users with unnecessary notifications, emails, or promotional content, increasing data traffic and server load for little added value.

Responsibility and Influence

Consumers are increasingly aware of their environmental impact, and they are actively seeking more sustainable options.[40] However, it is not reasonable to place the full burden of change on them. Companies have far greater influence on systemic change through product design, supply chain decisions, marketing strategy, and pricing structures.

Instead of maximising engagement or sales at any cost, companies must ask:

- Are we designing products and services that promote mindful use?
- Are we empowering users to make sustainable choices—or manipulating them to overconsume?
- Are we aligning our operations with environmental goals—or greenwashing?

A company's duty is to meet regulatory requirements or market trends and to

[40] Business Wire, 2021.

shape culture—and that includes creating the conditions for responsible consumption.

Shifting Expectations and Consumer Trust

A 2021 study by Business Wire[41] found that:

- 85 percent of consumers globally have shifted their behaviour towards sustainability in the last five years.
- 60 percent say sustainability is a key factor when making purchases.
- Many are even willing to abandon brands that do not align with their values.

Dr. Andreas von der Gathen, Co-CEO of Simon-Kucher, said sustainability will become even more central to purchasing decisions: "Today, 50 percent of consumers rank sustainability as a top five value driver."[42]

> *"As expectations around sustainability climb, companies will face significant pressure to prove their sustainability credentials and continue to make it a central part of their value proposition."*
>
> (Dr. Andreas von Gathen)

According to a study by Campaign Live[43], people believe that companies carry more responsibility than politicians. Consumers increasingly expect companies to take a stance and offer clear, authentic sustainability strategies—not just marketing slogans.

Conclusion: Shared Responsibility, Stronger Impact

Businesses have the responsibility to create sustainable and resource-conscious solutions. Whether physical goods like paper cups or digital services, short product lifespans harm efforts toward a sustainable circular economy. A throwaway culture has severe environmental consequences, exemplified by the *Pacific Garbage Patch*. This culture harms ecosystems, disrupts natural processes, and contributes to the long-term depletion of natural resources.

As societal expectations and consumer focus on sustainability continue to grow, companies must adapt their strategies to remain competitive. Increased responsibility will result in companies making stronger contributions to environmental protection.

3.3 Sustainability as a Competitive Advantage

In a world facing escalating environmental crises, dwindling natural resources, and growing societal demands, sustainability is no longer a "nice to have"—it is an essential requirement. Companies increasingly face the challenge of

---

[41] Business Wire, 2021.
[42] Business Wire, 2021.
[43] Campaign Live, 2016.

embedding sustainable practices throughout their business operations.

The change positively influences both strategy and regulation. Sustainability is becoming a key driver of innovation, competitiveness, and long-term value. While the transformation is complex, it offers companies new opportunities: improved risk management, stronger brand positioning, deeper customer loyalty, and increased attractiveness to investors[44] and talent alike.

Large corporations have long recognised this potential and have invested in ambitious sustainability initiatives. Now, small and medium-sized enterprises are also beginning to see that sustainability is not a burden, but a lever for future viability.

Corporate Initiatives: From CO_2-Neutral to Net Zero

Major companies are committing to bold sustainability goals:

- **Microsoft** aims to become carbon-negative by 2030 and to remove all historical emissions by 2050.[45]
- **Adobe** is targeting net-zero emissions by 2050, aligning its goals with the Paris Agreement's 1.5°C limit.[46]
- **Nvidia:** Investing in energy-efficient computing as a pathway to sustainability.[47]

CO_2-Emitting, CO_2-Neutral, Net-Zero, CO_2-Negative[48]

Carbon-emitting: Activities that release CO_2 into the atmosphere—such as burning fossil fuels or producing cement.
Carbon-neutral: Emissions are balanced by equivalent removal or offset measures.
Net-zero: All residual emissions are counterbalanced through carbon removal, resulting in no net climate impact.
Carbon-negative: More CO_2 is removed from the atmosphere than is emitted—through natural means (e.g. reforestation) or technology (e.g. direct air capture).

NVIDIA, a global leader in AI and graphics technology, emphasises energy-efficient computing as a lever for climate action. The concept is that more powerful processors use less energy to accomplish more tasks. However, this only holds if efficiency gains do not lead to a total increase in usage—a known risk referred to as the *Jevons Paradox*, where greater efficiency can paradoxically increase overall consumption.

---

[44] Ognen, Thomson, & Scores, 2018.
[45] Microsoft, 2024.
[46] Adobe, 2024.
[47] Nvidia, 2024.
[48] Erlach, et al., 2022.

NVIDIA's sustainability strategy reflects a strong commitment to both technological innovation and responsible resource use. The company actively integrates environmental stewardship with a focus on the needs and well-being of its employees. Being a UN Global Compact member, NVIDIA is committed to human rights and a broad array of ecological and social projects. This dedication has earned the company multiple independent awards and recognition as one of the top employers in the U.S.

Investment: Sustainability as a Value Driver

Investors increasingly consider sustainability a core factor, just as important as financial performance.[49] ESG ratings influence funding, valuations, and stakeholder trust. Companies integrating ESG principles benefit from:

- Increased market value
- Stronger customer retention
- Greater resilience to regulatory and reputational risk

3.4 Changing Consumer Behaviour

Consumer expectations are shifting rapidly. Sustainability is no longer a fringe concern or a bonus feature—it has become a key factor when making purchases, brand loyalty, and social identity. Today's customers are more informed, more discerning, and more willing to act on their values.[50]

According to studies by Capgemini[51] and Deloitte:[52]

- 79 percent of consumers seek to improve the planet.
- 72 percent are concerned about their environmental impact.
- 70 percent regularly opt for sustainable products when available.
- 60 percent feel emotionally better when buying from sustainable brands.
- 50 percent say they feel more connected to those brands.

These figures indicate a broader societal trend: people increasingly align purchasing decisions with personal values and environmental awareness. Consumers do not just buy a product—they buy what the brand stands for.

This behavioural shift is especially strong among younger generations. Millennials and Gen Z are more likely to:

- Question the origin and production conditions of products
- Demand transparency and traceability
- Engage with brands through social and environmental causes
- Publicly support or reject companies based on their sustainability record

Digital access makes this information easier to verify and share. Social media, product reviews, and watchdog platforms amplify consumer voices and

[49] Brosch & Schauerte, 2023; Lamont, 2022.
[50] KPMG, 2021.
[51] Capgemini, 2020.
[52] Deloitte Global, 2023.

allow sustainability claims to be scrutinised more closely than ever before. For businesses, this means that greenwashing is not only unethical—it is risky. Customers are quick to identify inconsistencies and call out performative branding. Authenticity, measurable action, and transparency are essential.

Companies that adapt and understand to these expectations position themselves as credible, future-oriented brands. They fulfil consumer demand and play a key role in shaping it. By offering genuinely sustainable alternatives, they empower customers to make better choices and build deeper emotional ties with the brand.

Ultimately, changing consumer behaviour is not just a reaction to market forces - it is a powerful signal: *sustainability has become mainstream*. And companies that listen, respond, and lead in this space will secure lasting relevance and trust.

3.5 Overcoming Corporate Doubts

Despite the growing importance of sustainability, many companies still have reservations. Common objections include high costs, limited resources, lack of regulatory clarity, and uncertainty about measurable benefits. The complexity and potential profit reduction associated with sustainability requirements may disproportionately burden small and medium-sized enterprises (SMEs).

According to Deloitte[53], about 25 percent of companies still cite costs as the main barrier to implementing sustainability initiatives. Beyond cost concerns, companies face several additional obstacles hindering their progress:

- Challenges in measuring environmental impact
- A short-term focus driven by investor or shareholder expectations
- Lack of political support or structural enablers, such as green infrastructure or investment incentives
- Conflicting or unclear regulatory and reporting frameworks
- A limited long-term view of the values of sustainability to their business

> The key question is: *Why do we focus on the cost of sustainability instead of asking what it will cost if we do nothing?*

However, these concerns are increasingly being disproven in practice. Studies, like Deloitte Global[54] and real-world examples, like below, show that companies with strong sustainability strategies improve their environmental and social performance while also gaining tangible business advantages—such as stronger customer loyalty, more motivated employees, better risk management, and improved long-term resilience.

Svenja Stöveken, a strategy expert at Horváth, argues that the concern about sustainability harming the business model is outdated. In her view,

[53] Deloitte Global, 2023.
[54] Deloitte Global, 2023.

sustainability is not a cost factor, but an essential enabler of future viability. Acting early allows companies to influence markets, achieve competitive edge, and foster trust.[55]

Similarly, Eelco Smit, Senior Director of Sustainability at Philips, challenges the outdated assumption that sustainability compromises profitability. Drawing on Philips' own experience with sustainable product design and responsible supply chains. He insists that sustainability and profitability can go hand in hand. The Sustainable Brand Index, along with niche providers, shows that consumers are increasingly rewarding sustainable brands. This shift has encouraged more companies to invest in sustainability. He dismisses the idea that sustainability always comes at a cost or reduces profitability, calling it outdated. Instead, he emphasises the need to move beyond that mindset.[56]

Smit's point is critical: sustainability is no longer a marketing feature—it is a strategic foundation for long-term business survival. Customers expect meaningful action, and increasingly, so do investors and employees.

In short: waiting poses greater risks than acting. Even small, transparent steps—like energy optimisation, circular design principles, or sustainable packaging—can build trust and competitive strength. What matters is a clear commitment, authenticity, and continuous improvement.

Best Practices – Adidas, Unilever, and Schneider Electric

Many global companies demonstrate that integrating sustainability into products, processes, and company culture can drive business success. These companies show that sustainability is not a side project, but a core business strategy.

Adidas's commitment to sustainability spans over two decades, actively integrating sustainability goals into business planning.[57] In collaboration with the environmental organisation *Parley for the Oceans*, Adidas has been producing shoes made from recycled ocean plastic since 2015. What started as a niche initiative has grown into a global product line: from 15 million pairs in 2020[58] to 27 million in 2022.[59] This growth reflects increasing consumer demand for eco-friendly alternatives and has also helped the company reduce its material footprint. Former CEO Kasper Rorsted pointed to a shift in consumer values: according to Adidas data, 70 percent of customers consider sustainability a key factor in their purchase decisions.[60] By turning waste into value, Adidas meets expectations while also strengthening its brand purpose and image of innovation.

---

[55] Stöveken & Brugger, 2018.
[56] Deloitte, 2023.
[57] Adidas, 2022.
[58] Rorsted, 2021.
[59] Adidas, 2023.
[60] Rorsted, 2021.

Unilever, one of the world's largest producers of consumer goods, has systematically integrated sustainability into its business model. Under the umbrella of its *Sustainable Living Plan*, brands like Dove, Ben & Jerry's, and Lipton have adopted goals for reducing emissions, improving social impact, and enhancing transparency. The result: Unilever's "Sustainable Living Brands" are growing nearly twice as fast as its other brands—and contributed to about 70 percent of total company growth.[61] This success confirms what studies repeatedly show: authentic and visible implementation of sustainability strengthens market performance and customer relationships.

Schneider Electric, a global specialist in energy management and automation, has embedded sustainability into the core of the company's business strategy. The company's open platform *EcoStruxure*, for example, helps businesses monitor and optimise energy use, reduce emissions, and increase operational efficiency. Besides developing energy-saving technologies, Schneider also addresses systemic sustainability through biodiversity programs, generational collaboration, and plastic reduction initiatives. Schneider Electric has received multiple recognitions as one of the world's most sustainable companies and serves as a model for combining technology and environmental responsibility.[62]

3.6 Sustainability as a Talent Magnet

Sustainability is transforming products, supply chains, and markets—but is also reshaping the *job market*. For many professionals, particularly younger generations, environmental and social responsibility are now essential criteria when choosing an employer. Companies that prioritise sustainability gain a critical competitive edge in the search for talent.

Study of European Invest Bank shows that over 80 percent of Gen Z and Millennials in Germany actively research a company's environmental impact and values before applying.[63] They expect transparency, purpose, and genuine commitment. In this context, sustainability becomes more than an HR trend: it is a decisive factor in employer branding and workforce loyalty.

A strong sense of purpose in the workplace fosters motivation, engagement, and innovation. Employees who feel that their company contributes to a larger mission—like climate protection or social justice—are more likely to stay, perform better, and advocate for the brand.

The demand for sustainability-specific roles is growing rapidly. Companies are hiring sustainability officers, circular economy specialists, ESG analysts, and UX designers focused on environmental impact. This creates new career paths—and new expectations for corporate culture.

The organisation must live and visibly show sustainable values in all aspects,

[61] Unilever, 2019.
[62] Time, 2024; Corporate Knights, 2025.
[63] Europäische Investitionsbank, 2023.

from job postings and onboarding to internal communication and leadership. This includes:

- Sustainable office practices (e.g. energy use, mobility, digital infrastructure)
- Social equity and inclusive leadership
- Clear sustainability goals and transparent reporting

Companies that meet these expectations not only attract high-potential candidates—they build future-proof teams that identify with their mission.

3.7 Summary and Conclusion

Sustainability is no longer a sideline or marketing bonus—it is a core strategic imperative. Companies that embed environmental and social responsibility into their business models position themselves as ethical actors and future-ready innovators.

The examples of Adidas, Unilever, and Schneider Electric show how sustainability, when treated as a central driver rather than an obligation, leads to growth, resilience, and competitive advantage. These organisations prove that aligning purpose with profit works, demonstrating how ecological and economic goals support each other.

The benefits are multifaceted:

- Stronger customer loyalty through transparent, value-driven action
- Increased investor appeal and access to ESG-driven capital
- Increased innovation, driven by new materials, business models, and digital tools
- Attraction and retaining top talent, especially from younger generations
- Improved risk management in the face of climate, regulatory, and reputational challenges

Meanwhile, the consequences of inaction are growing. Companies that delay their sustainability transformation risk falling behind—in market relevance and in talent recruitment, financing, and long-term viability.

Strategic sustainability is therefore not about perfection—it is about direction, consistency, and the willingness to act. Companies recognising this will act early and remain transparent in their journey to better shape the future—ecologically, socially, and economically.

4 HOW USER EXPERIENCE AFFECTS THE TARGET AUDIENCE

Digital products shape user behaviour and perception—sometimes subtly, sometimes in powerful ways. Design influences whether users perceive a digital experience as helpful, frustrating, or inspiring. Between "positive" and "negative" experiences lies a spectrum of user reactions, from "rather yes" to "rather no." A well-designed user experience fosters satisfaction, trust, and engagement. The consequences of poor UX include user frustration, high drop-off rates, and reputational damage. Understanding the needs, expectations, and goals of the target audience is essential—and must be consistently embedded in the design process.

4.1 Conventional User Experience

User-centered design focuses on making digital products intuitive, accessible, and efficient. When applied consistently, it leads to experiences that are functional and enjoyable.

A conventional, well-implemented user experience typically includes being:

- Efficient and effective
- Accessible
- Visually appealing
- Intuitive an Functional
- Based on user needs

This focus brings several measurable benefits:

- **Higher satisfaction:** Users feel comfortable when they intuitively understand how to navigate a product.
- **Stronger user loyalty**: A positive experience encourages repeat use and fosters long-term retention.
- **Positive brand perception**: A smooth digital experience reflects on the brand—enhancing its image as innovative and customer-focused.
- **Higher conversion rates**: When goals are simple to achieve, users are more likely to act—whether buying, subscribing, or contacting.
- **Lower frustration levels**: A clear interface reduces mental effort and prevents drop-offs.
- **Competitive advantage**: In saturated markets, a thoughtful UX can be a key differentiator.

Example 1: Conventional UX in E-Commerce

An online clothing retailer offers a seamless user experience: intuitive navigation, a streamlined checkout, and fast delivery. Users appreciate the efficiency and convenience—and are motivated to return. This ensures a consistently positive user experience.

4.2 How Sustainability Enriches UX

Building on a strong UX, integrating sustainability principles takes user experience to the next level. It adds meaning, purpose, and ethical value to the interaction.

A sustainable UX design is:

- Environmentally friendly and resource-efficient
- Long-lasting
- Transparent and ethically correct
- Inclusive and socially responsible
- Diverse
- Economically beneficial

When sustainability becomes part of the design language, additional user benefits emerge:

- **Greater trust and credibility**: Brands that act responsibly build long-term relationships.
- **Appeal to eco-conscious users**: A growing segment prefers products aligned with their values.
- **Stronger emotional connection**: Sustainability fosters identification with the brand beyond functionality.
- **Clear brand differentiation**: Ethical design stands out in competitive markets.
- **Raising awareness and modelling values**: Sustainable experiences foster awareness and values, guiding users to act more mindfully.
- **Efficient use of resources**: Lean digital solutions save data, time, and energy—benefiting both the environment and business.
- **Transparency and accountability**: Communicating sustainability efforts openly builds user trust and sets a positive example.

Example 2: Sustainable UX in Practice

Building on Example 1, the same retailer further develops its platform by integrating clear sustainability measures. The website now displays detailed information about clothing origins, material composition, and the fair working conditions behind production. The team has optimised the site's architecture for energy efficiency, reducing data load and server usage. During the checkout process, customers have the option to offset the CO_2 emissions from their shipment, with contributions supporting certified environmental projects. Additionally, the company has redesigned its packaging to be both minimal and environmentally friendly.

As a result, customers enjoy a smooth and intuitive shopping experience, and additionally they feel aligned with the brand's ethical values. They recognise that the company acts responsibly both socially and environmentally and this strengthens their trust and emotional connection. This fosters a strong sense of connection and loyalty, leading them to choose the same company for their next purchase.

4.3 Conclusion

User experience plays a central role in digital product development—enabling people to interact with systems intuitively, efficiently, and with satisfaction. However, as environmental and social challenges continue to grow, this definition no longer reflects the broader needs of both people and the planet.

People seek functional and enjoyable experiences, as well as alignment with their personal values and a deeper sense of purpose. When companies embed sustainability into user experience design, they meet practical needs while also addressing a deeper emotional layer: the desire to act responsibly and support brands that take ownership of their impact.

Sustainable UX introduces a new dimension of engagement—one rooted in awareness, responsibility, and long-term value. This approach empowers users to make informed choices, reduces digital and material waste, and embodies principles of transparency, fairness, and environmental stewardship. Through these practices, sustainable UX strengthens trust—in the product and in the brand behind it.

Integrating sustainability into design lets companies support societal goals like climate protection, social justice, and digital inclusion, without affecting usability or competitiveness. They create differentiation, drive innovation, and build lasting relationships with a more conscious customer base.

The combination of usability and responsibility produces a powerful effect, turning digital interfaces into meaningful experiences and brands into ethical partners. Sustainable UX is not a trend—*it is the future of design*. By embracing this shift, companies enhance user lives and actively shape a more responsible digital future.

5 HOW CAN WE RAISE AWARENESS OF SUSTAINABILITY?

Anyone who has ever travelled in Asian countries may have noticed a special feature at various intersections: traffic lights equipped with countdown timers. Thailand, for example, has been using this system for years. These traffic lights display the exact number of seconds remaining until the light changes from red to green or vice versa. This small design decision has a notable effect—reducing stress and impatience among drivers. But its influence goes further: studies have shown that such transparency improves road safety and lowers emissions.[64] Because people know how long they have to wait, they brake less abruptly, accelerate more smoothly, and adjust their driving more consciously.

How does this relate to sustainability and user experience?

The countdown timer illustrates a fundamental truth: *when information is clear, timely, and visible, it shapes behaviour*—often without users even realising the influence. The countdown timer makes invisible time visible, leading to safer and more environmentally friendly decisions. This principle translates directly into the digital realm: effective user experience design makes the consequences of an action transparent, tangible, and relevant. And that is exactly what is needed: awareness of sustainability.

Many sustainability challenges, like climate change, pollution, and social inequality, are abstract, long-term, or geographically distant. They do not trigger immediate concern. People are far more likely to respond to immediate threats or changes but struggle to link their own behaviour with distant or long-term consequences.

> *"People often use simplistic and linear logic and think only of immediate results, not long-term consequences."*
>
> (Norman, 2023, p. 239)

Constant confrontation with such impacts is urgently needed to overcome this gap. The communication of sustainability influences people's willingness to act responsibly. When design makes environmental impact visible and personally relevant, it activates reflection and responsibility. UX helps to close

[64] Islam et al., 2017; Minjeong & Hoe, 2020; Santos, Ribeiro, Metrôlho, & Dionísio, 2024.

this gap by embedding sustainability into everyday digital interactions. Through clear communication, feedback systems, and emotional engagement, design has the power to make users aware of their impact and empower them to make better choices.

The following sections explore the psychological and behavioural foundations of awareness-building, show how digital design promotes reflection and responsibility, and provide practical tools to encourage responsible behaviour—ethically, effectively, and without manipulation.

5.1 Inside the Mind: Thinking and Decision Processes

Communication of sustainability plays a crucial role in motivating people to make environmentally responsible choices. UX design makes abstract concepts such as climate change, biodiversity loss, or resource scarcity tangible through interactive design elements, feedback loops, or gamified features. However, this requires a solid understanding of how people think and decide.

Anyone familiar with psychological models of human cognition will have encountered Daniel Kahneman's model of *System 1* and *System 2* thinking. Less known but equally insightful is Don Norman's theory of *three levels of thinking*. Together, these frameworks offer a holistic foundation for designing sustainable user experiences that engage both instinct and reflection.

Daniel Kahneman's Systems Thinking

In *Thinking, Fast and Slow*[65], Nobel laureate Daniel Kahneman identifies two modes of thought:

- **System 1** is fast, automatic, and intuitive. It uses little effort, and people often use it for routine actions such as driving a familiar route or responding to visual stimuli.
- **System 2** is slow, analytical, and deliberate. It is engaged when solving complex problems, making new decisions, or evaluating consequences.

Example:

Driving, shifting gears, or braking typically happens through System 1—almost unconsciously. In contrast, unfamiliar or complex traffic situations (e.g. driving in extreme weather conditions, like heavy snow) activate System 2.

Kahneman focuses on general cognitive processes and human decision-making across a variety of contexts through his two-system theory. His goal is to explain the mechanisms behind fast and slow thinking, and how these influence decisions. This approach is valuable for understanding and shaping the cognitive aspects of human interaction. Understanding this dichotomy

[65] Kahneman, 2011.

helps designers distinguish between habitual behaviour and conscious decision-making—both crucial for sustainable interaction design.

Don Norman's Perspectives: How People Perceive and React

While Daniel Kahneman's model helps explain how people think, Don Norman focuses on *how people experience* the world around them. In his book *Emotional Design*,[66] Norman identifies three levels of cognitive processing that influence how we interact with the world—and, by extension, with digital products:

Visceral Thinking

At the visceral level, users respond with immediate, instinctive emotions to sensory input—what something looks, sounds, or feels like. For example, the visual language of a website—its colours, layout, typography, or motion—evokes a gut-level response. Calming colours, balanced spacing, and clean typography in digital products subtly convey calmness, trustworthiness, and environmental awareness to users before content interaction. This first impression, although subconscious, significantly shapes the willingness to engage.

Behaviour-Based Thinking

On the behavioural level, thinking corresponds to routine actions and habits that become automatic through repetition and practice. These are goal-directed activities performed with little conscious effort, such as riding a bicycle, typing on a keyboard, or preparing a familiar meal. This type of thinking enables efficient action by relying on learned patterns and feedback, without placing significant demands on cognitive resources.

Sustainable UX supports user at this level by embedding environmentally conscious behaviours—like choosing low-emission delivery options or digital receipts—into familiar interaction flows. When these options align with users' habitual behaviour, they are more likely to be adopted simply because they fit naturally and require minimal effort.

Reflective Thinking

At the reflective level, users become consciously analytical, stepping back to evaluate their behaviour. They ask themselves questions: Is this the right decision? Do I support this company's values? What does this say about me? This is the level at which users care deeply about a product's ethical and environmental context.

UX design addresses this by offering transparency about the product's impact, providing background stories or certifications, and allowing users to track their own sustainability-related contributions. We build loyalty in this

[66] Normann, 2004.

reflective space—to the product and to its purpose.

Building on the Example Above

Take driving as an example: we can expand Kahneman's theory by introducing an experiential precursor—a clean, pleasantly scented car that enhances the driving experience by subconsciously evoking a sense of well-being and satisfaction. These visceral impressions operate on a level prior to conscious perception and play a central role in shaping user experience by fostering an emotional connection to the product.

Applying the Models to UX Design

Promoting sustainable behaviour through UX requires addressing both intuitive and conscious processes. The application of Kahneman's and Norman's models can be structured into:

- **Unconscious (visceral) design**: Uses natural colour palettes (e.g. green, blue), nature imagery, and emotionally resonant aesthetics to establish a positive first impression of sustainability before the user engages or decides.
- **Intuitive (behavioural) design**: Facilitates effortless sustainable actions—such as pre-selected CO_2-neutral shipping options, gamified incentives for conscious behaviour, and clearly marked sustainable choices using familiar icons or colour codes.
- **Conscious (reflective) design**: Encourages deeper engagement by showing CO_2 savings, visualising long-term progress, and offering detailed background info. This fosters reflection and strengthens informed decision-making.

Although Norman's and Kahneman's approaches emphasise different aspects of cognition, they complement one another and together offer a comprehensive understanding of how people think and act. Kahneman distinguishes between fast, unconscious thought (System 1) and slow, reflective reasoning (System 2).

Norman focuses on the visceral, behavioural, and reflective levels, especially in product interaction and user experience. Kahneman emphasises the cognitive dimensions of thinking, while Norman also incorporates emotional and sensory processing. Together, their models form a holistic perspective—one that considers everything from automatic impulses and ingrained routines to conscious, value-driven decisions.

The Practical Use of Kahneman and Norman's Models

Applying these models to UX design prompts a key question: *How can we encourage sustainable choices through user behaviour and thinking?*

To foster sustainable behaviour, UX design must engage both the intuitive and the reflective mind. Kahneman and Norman's insights allow us to develop design strategies applicable to unconscious, intuitive, and conscious cognitive processing.

Unconscious Thinking (aka Visceral Level)

Unconscious, or visceral thinking, speaks to people's immediate, emotional reactions. Here, we anchor sustainability at a sensory level. Thoughtful visual and aesthetic design—featuring clean, modern interfaces, natural colours like green or blue, and imagery evoking nature, balance, or harmony—establishes a positive baseline emotional response. Even before users make an active choice, these emotional cues shape their perception. A digital product that "feels sustainable" sets the stage for deeper engagement.

Intuitive Thinking (aka System 1 / Behavioural Level)

Intuitive thinking is fast, automatic, and effortless. It responds best to familiar patterns, simple choices, and visual clarity. Sustainable UX at this level enables low-effort, high-impact actions. Pre-selecting sustainable delivery options by default, for example, guides users toward eco-friendly choices. Symbols and colour codes instantly highlight sustainable alternatives. Gamification elements—such as points, badges, or progress bars linked to sustainable actions—motivate continued engagement without requiring deep reflection. These features embed sustainable behaviour into daily routines, making eco-friendly choices the easiest and most natural choice.

Conscious Thinking (aka System 2 / Reflective Level)

Conscious thinking requires more time and attention. Users activate this level when they reflect on their decisions and consider consequences. To activate it, UX design should provide transparent, trustworthy information. For instance, showing real-time CO_2 savings or visualising a user's cumulative environmental impact over time can foster deeper awareness. By linking individual behaviour with long-term ecological outcomes, reflective design helps users internalise sustainable values and strengthens their emotional commitment to conscious choices.

Conclusion

These models make it clear: a multi-layered design approach leads to truly sustainable user experiences. By addressing visceral, behavioural, and reflective dimensions—or, in Kahneman's terms, both System 1 and System 2 thinking—UX design promotes immediate sustainable actions and fosters lasting behaviour change.

5.2 Behaviour Management Frameworks

Understanding and actively shaping human behaviour lies at the core of two influential models: behavioural design and the Hook Model[67]. Both draw on behavioural science and psychology to show how intentionally structured environments and interactions drive behaviour change, build habits, and support long-term engagement. Purposeful use of psychological insights makes sustainable decisions easier and shapes digital experiences that support conscious action.

Behavioural Design

Behavioural design seeks to guide human behaviour by creating environments and interactions that make desired actions feel simple, intuitive, and attractive. This approach builds on findings from psychology, neuroscience, and behavioural economics to develop strategies that support change at both the individual and societal levels.

One of the most influential models in this field is the Behaviour Model developed by B. J. Fogg, behavioural scientist, and founder of the Behaviour Design Lab at Stanford University.

> *"A behavior happens when the three elements of MAP—Motivation, Ability, and Prompt—come together at the same moment."*
>
> (Fogg, 2020)

Behaviour occurs, per Fogg's model, when three factors are present together:

Motivation

Motivation refers to a person's desire to act—whether driven by intrinsic values, such as environmental concern, or extrinsic rewards, such as savings or recognition. Designing for behaviour change begins with understanding what drives people and using that insight to address their motivations in respectful, effective ways.

Ability

Ability reflects how simple or difficult it is to perform a behaviour. Even highly motivated individuals may not act if the behaviour feels too complex or out of reach. Sustainable UX simplifies processes, removes barriers, and equips users with the tools and guidance.

Trigger

A trigger (or prompt) is the cue that initiates behaviour—such as a notification, visual element, question, or social reminder. Effective triggers are well-timed and placed in contexts where the user is motivated and able to act.

---

[67] Eyal, 2014.

The power of Fogg's model lies in its simplicity and applicability. Whether the goal is reducing energy consumption, encouraging climate-neutral shopping, or promoting digital minimalism—if motivation, ability, and a clear prompt are present simultaneously, sustainable behaviour becomes far more likely.

Conclusion

Behavioural design plays a key role in shaping digital applications that positively influence behaviour. When scientific insight meets creative design, even targeted adjustments drive meaningful change benefiting both individuals and society. The method developed by B. J. Fogg provides a solid foundation for understanding target audiences and creating effective, sustainable solutions. Thoughtful, well-placed changes have the power to generate significant progress on both a personal and societal level.

The Hook Model: Forming Habits in a Targeted Manner

The Hook Model, developed by Nir Eyal[68], explains how habits form and strengthen through a repeatable four-step cycle. It engages users in a continuous loop of behaviour driven by strategic triggers, purposeful actions, variable rewards, and user investment. Product designers apply this model to keep users and foster consistent engagement.

In a sustainability context, adapting the Hook Model helps promote environmentally conscious actions and integrates them into everyday life—eventually forming lasting habits.

The model unfolds in four phases:

Trigger

External triggers come from the outside—such as notifications or reminders that prompt a specific action. In contrast, internal triggers stem from emotions, routines, or memories, such as boredom, loneliness, or a need for social interaction.

Actions

At this stage, users take the intended action. The actions must be clear, effortless, and satisfying to complete. In sustainable UX, actions include, for example, one-click switches to eco-friendly options or seamless submission of digital return forms to reduce waste.

Variable rewards

Variable rewards are essential for habit formation. They meet an existing need while simultaneously generating anticipation and curiosity about the next interaction. These rewards may be social—such as recognition or approval—or intrinsic, like achieving a personal goal or solving a meaningful problem. In

[68] Eyal, 2014.

sustainable UX, such rewards might include progress feedback, community recognition, personalised eco-points, or impactful stories, all aimed at maintaining long-term user motivation.

Investment

Investment strengthens user commitment by encouraging contributions of time, effort, data, or money. Examples include creating a profile, uploading content, or completing a subscription. These acts deepen the emotional connection to the product or behaviour and increase the likelihood of continued engagement.

Example

Marie regularly shops at an online store that sells sustainable products. At regular intervals, she receives push notifications about new eco-friendly items. This time, the notification reads: "Plastic-free—discover sustainable alternatives for your everyday life."

She taps the notification and browses the offers and buys a product she had been looking for—a simple purchase she completes quickly. Afterward, the store sends a message thanking her for contributing meaningfully to reducing plastic waste. It also includes a statistic showing the impact of her choice.

To her delight, the company awards eco-points for purchases like this, which she can use for future orders. These rewards encourage her to continue shopping sustainably. Motivated, Marie writes a positive review and shares her experience with her community. Fellow members recognise her contribution, strengthening her connection with both the community and the brand.

Conclusion

The Hook Model offers a powerful framework for shaping habits and fostering long-term engagement. But it also carries risks: businesses may misuse it for manipulation or exploitation. Overuse, overconsumption, and overreliance on digital platforms remain real dangers. That is why ethical companies take responsibility for applying the model transparently and thoughtfully prioritising long-term user well-being over short-term gains.

5.3 Behavioural Design Method for Promoting Sustainable Digital Practices

Promoting sustainable behaviour requires methods that specifically address how people decide and act. Psychological, narrative, and design-based strategies help create a context in which responsible choices for the planet become easier, more appealing, and more rewarding. Techniques such as green nudging, storytelling, and green by default have proven especially effective in motivating sustainable behaviour in everyday digital interactions.

Green Nudging: Gentle Prompts for Sustainability

Incentives play a critical role in behaviour change. They highlight progress, reinforce habits, and create a sense of satisfaction. One particularly influential strategy is nudging—a concept that involves subtle prompts or design elements that steer people toward beneficial behaviour without restricting their freedom of choice.

The term "nudging," introduced by Richard Thaler and Cass Sunstein in 2008, refers to small design interventions that encourage behavioural shifts[69]—for example, lowering energy consumption—without relying on bans or financial penalties. The underlying principle, known as *libertarian paternalism*, combines free decision-making with interventions that support people's long-term well-being. Using nudging specifically to encourage climate-friendly or sustainable behaviour makes it *green nudging*.

Green nudges are minor design changes that make environmentally friendly actions more appealing or easier to execute—without removing alternatives. For example, the German National Climate Initiative (NKI)[70] conducted a project in which companies tested green nudges such as visual cues, default settings, and intentionally designed decision pathways. The goal was to reduce paper consumption, promote energy-saving behaviour, and encourage responsible commuting. These nudges drew on psychological incentives and behavioural science to promote climate-friendly behaviour without limiting individual freedom of choice. The measures, tested across several companies and Organisations, revealed that such interventions positively influence behaviour and effectively support responsible decision-making.

Examples of green nudging in digital UX include:

- Setting climate-friendly delivery as the default, with the option to change it
- Highlighting eco-friendly products with labels such as "eco" or "climate-friendly"
- Offering the option to reduce or eliminate packaging during checkout
- Recommending more sustainable alternatives in the shopping cart
- Displaying the carbon footprint of products next to the price
- Providing digital invoices by default while still offering paper on request
- Informing users about the environmental cost of returns to reduce unnecessary shipments

Conclusion

Green nudging makes sustainable behaviour easier and more likely. It raises environmental awareness without creating pressure and leaves users fully in

[69] Thaler & Sunstein, 2008.
[70] ConPolicy, 2020.

control of their choices.

Storytelling: Shaping Sustainable UX Through Narrative

Storytelling is a powerful method for conveying complex information in a simple, emotional, and memorable way. It creates immersive experiences that tap into both rational understanding and emotional responses. Neuroscience and communication studies reveal that narratives powerfully boost attention, comprehension, and engagement.[71] When applied to sustainability, storytelling helps transform abstract ecological or social issues into relatable and motivating narratives.

Instead of communicating sustainability through isolated facts or numerical values alone, narratives allow users to emotionally connect with a cause, understand the "why," and feel part of a bigger picture.

Example 1

A company that successfully reduced its CO_2 emissions by half could present this achievement not as a static number, but through a visual storytelling format. An interactive timeline could illustrate the journey—from identifying the problem, to implementing changes, to achieving tangible results. Users experience the process as a story of transformation.

Example 2

A fashion brand might tell the story of a garment's journey: from harvesting organic cotton to production in factories that ensure fair wages and safe working conditions. The product becomes more than fabric—it becomes a story of values. This emotional lens increases the chance that customers will choose sustainable options and feel good about doing so.

Example 3

A sustainable online retailer might use gamified storytelling to visualise impact. For example, when a user selects a climate-friendly shipping option, a virtual tree meadow grows on screen. Users watch their forest grow as they make eco-conscious decisions. This form of narrative feedback strengthens positive behaviour while creating a shared story between user and brand.

Conclusion

Storytelling is more than a marketing tool—it is a medium for movement and meaning. In sustainable UX, it combines rational information with emotional resonance, turning sustainability from a technical attribute into a lived

[71] Szyszka, 2024; Ameseder & Ettl-Huber, 2017.

experience. Stories make sustainability ***graspable, tangible***, and ***memorable***. They empower users to move from understanding to action—embedding values into everyday behaviour and fostering a meaningful sense of participation in building a more sustainable and responsible future.

Green by Default

Imagine a world where everyday life is shaped by sustainability—not as an extra, but as the starting point. Electric vehicles silence the streets. Solar panels gleam on rooftops. Green oases flourish between buildings, with climbing plants and trees turning city parks into miniature forests. Even your morning coffee arrives in compostable packaging—not because you chose it, but because that is simply the standard. Plastic waste? A thing of the past.

This vision, though seemingly utopian, is possible; especially once sustainability becomes the standard within our systems, not a choice.

Green by Default

Green by default means prioritising sustainability as the standard. This behavioural design strategy promotes environmentally friendly choices by setting them as the *default option*, which simplifies decision-making and reduces cognitive load for users.[72] People keep full freedom of choice, but they often follow the sustainable path because the system has already selected that option.

The "default effect" is a well-documented phenomenon in behavioural economics. People tend to stick with preset options, especially when changing them requires extra effort. Green defaults capitalise on this tendency, using it ethically to nudge behaviour toward sustainability.

Real-World Applications

There are many ways to implement "green by default." Companies may offer recyclable packaging as the default setting. Websites can pre-select climate-neutral shipping options. Governments might mandate renewable energy contracts for public buildings and households unless users actively choose another option.

A striking example comes from a study in Switzerland:[73] energy providers set green electricity as the default option for over 200,000 households and 8,000 companies. Although switching to cheaper conventional tariffs was readily available, about *80 percent* of participants stayed with the green alternative—despite its higher cost. This underscores the transformative power of default settings to scale sustainable behaviour.

[72] Ramirez, 2020.
[73] Liebe et al., 2021.

Conclusion

The “green by default” strategy is more than a convenience—it is a systemic lever. By embedding sustainable practices into default configurations, we promote responsible choices and reduce decision fatigue, and lower the threshold for action. In the long term, such approaches lead to profound structural changes, normalising sustainability across sectors and making it part of everyday life.

5.4 Ethical Responsibility: Between Freedom and Influence

The common goal of behavioural design, the Hook Model, green nudging, storytelling, and the “green by default” approach is to positively influence human behaviour. These strategies use behavioural psychology and design research and subtly guide decision-making or promote desired actions. Yet, given their far-reaching impact, one aspect is becoming increasingly central in the design discourse: *the ethical dimension*.

This leads to a fundamental question: To what extent do these interventions respect ethical boundaries? Where do we draw the line between guiding behaviour and preserving individual autonomy? The core challenge lies in balancing the potential benefits of these strategies with the need to protect users’ freedom of choice.

Ethical design plays a key role in ensuring that behaviour-shaping methods remain both effective and morally legitimate. As Liebe et al.[74] argue in their article about effects of green energy defaults, behaviour change through design is justifiable only when it aligns with the individual's interests and respects their autonomy.

Transparency

An ethical approach to UX relies on full transparency. Users must understand design’s impact on their actions. This clarity helps them maintain autonomy and make informed decisions. For example, an app that encourages sustainable choices explains how those choices benefit the environment and reflect shared societal values. With this understanding, users act voluntarily and with awareness.

Voluntariness

The ability to steer behaviour through UX design always carries a risk of manipulation. Nudging or pressuring people into actions they would not choose with full awareness undermines ethical practice. Tactics like artificial scarcity (“Only a few items left!”), urgency messaging (“Buy now!”), or countdown timers often trigger impulsive behaviour.[75] Companies use these methods to drive sales, but they cross ethical boundaries when they undermine

---

[74] Liebe et al., 2021.

[75] Typical examples of FOMO (Fear of Missing Out).

user autonomy or disrupt thoughtful decision-making.

> *"Manipulation is directly influencing someone's beliefs, desires, or emotions, such that she falls short of ideals for belief, desire, or emotion in ways typically not in her self-interest or likely not in her self-interest in the present context."*
>
> (Barnhill, 2014)

Therefore, companies and designers should focus on empowering users to make independent decisions—building long-term trust and sustainable engagement, instead of confusing them with manipulative tactics.

Protection of Vulnerable Groups

An important aspect of ethical design involves protecting vulnerable groups. Children, adolescents, older adults, and people with disabilities or mental health challenges are more susceptible to subtle persuasive techniques used in digital platforms and services. Designers need to create UX mechanisms—such as green nudging or habit-forming features—in a way that avoids exploitation and prevents unintended harm. These approaches empower users while ensuring accessibility and fairness in every interaction.

Ethical Design as Opportunity

Ethical UX is not a restriction—it is an *opportunity*. It allows companies to merge innovation with moral values and to create added value both socially and commercially. Brands that take ethical responsibility seriously strengthen user trust, foster loyalty, and establish long-term relationships grounded in shared principles.

Ultimately, the role of design is to critically reflect on the consequences of their actions and to ensure that behavioural influence is both functional and fair. Ethical design means shaping change in a way that generates lasting benefits for users, society, and the planet—compromising no one's freedom to choose.

5.5 Summary and Critical Reflection

This chapter shows how thoughtful design and targeted communication encourage sustainable behaviour. Drawing on psychological frameworks developed by Kahneman and Norman, the discussion shows how design addresses both unconscious responses and deliberate decisions. Designers support sustainable behaviour by combining intuitive patterns, reflective information, and structural choices—such as setting sustainable options as the default ("Green by Default").

However, these behavioural strategies come with ethical obligations. Models such as Fogg's Behavior Model and Eyal's Hook Model provide powerful frameworks for influencing user behaviour. This influence, however, also brings risk: without transparency, these methods can manipulate rather than empower. Ethical design practices require open communication, voluntary user participation, and attention to the needs of vulnerable groups.

A major challenge in applying such strategies emerges in the Jevons Paradox. This phenomenon describes how increased efficiency or improved sustainable offerings do not always lead to reduced consumption; in fact, they can result in higher overall usage. For instance, when climate-neutral shipping becomes the default, users often place more orders, viewing them as harmless—yet the net environmental impact may grow. This leads to a key insight: making sustainable choices easier does not guarantee meaningful change. UX design also needs to promote critical reflection and help users became aware of the broader consequences of their actions. Real progress requires more than simplification—it relies on education and engagement.

Sustainable user experience design works best when it makes environmentally responsible behaviour accessible, intuitive, and personally meaningful. When decisions align ease with ethics, UX design drives change—both in individual behaviour and in building a more sustainable society.

6 THE THREE PILLARS OF SUSTAINABLE UX–PEOPLE, PLANET, AND PROFIT

Sustainability in user experience is not one-dimensional. It comprises three interconnected dimensions: *ecological*, *social*, and *economic* sustainability. This three-pillar model has developed over several decades, shaped by major international frameworks such as the Brundtland Report (1987)[76], the Rio Declaration (1992)[77], and John Elkington's Triple Bottom Line[78] in the 1990s.

Within digital product development, sustainability means designing for usability and performance, and also regarding long-term consequences for people, the planet, and business. This integrated perspective promotes responsible innovation and supports the creation of future-ready digital systems.

Sustainable UX means integrating these dimensions into every step of the design process:

- **User research**: Investigate user needs, behaviours, and the broader context–social, environmental, and cultural–that shapes their experiences. Use interviews, observations, and participatory methods to uncover deeper insights and identify potential unintended consequences.
- **Concept development**: Set clear ethical and sustainability goals based on research findings. Align design concepts with values such as fairness, environmental responsibility, and long-term social benefits. Ensure each idea supports user empowerment and contributes to systemic well-being.
- **Design phase**: Create inclusive, accessible, and resource-conscious solutions. Focus on clarity, usability, and visual balance while minimising cognitive load and environmental impact. Integrate strategies like green nudging and sustainable defaults to support conscious user behaviour.
- **Implementation**: Use energy-efficient, scalable technologies and adopt sustainable coding practices during development. Collaborate with cross-functional teams to minimise environmental impact across production and operation. Ensure that technical execution reflects the project's ethical and sustainability objectives.
- **Evaluation**: Test with real users to assess social, environmental, and

[76] Brundtland, 1987.
[77] United Nations, 1993.
[78] Elkington, 1997.

economic impact. Identify areas to improve usability, minimise unintended harm, and increase long-term value. Use direct feedback and measurable outcomes to guide continuous improvement.

6.1 Ecological Sustainability: Efficient and Future-Ready

Ecological sustainability focuses on reducing the environmental footprint of digital products and services. The scope includes energy use, data quantity, materials consumption, and devices' lifecycles.

A powerful example is the environmental cost of global email traffic. With over 350 billion emails sent daily, the energy required to process, store, and transmit them is enormous.[79] Even spam emails or short emails, though automatically filtered, generate CO_2 emissions—each one adding an average of about 0.03 grams of CO_2.[80] These numbers increase exponentially, especially as senders distribute millions of unnecessary messages.

In response, a UK campaign introduced a simple but powerful message: *"Think before you thank."*[81] Avoiding unnecessary confirmation emails helps to reduce digital carbon footprints. Common examples of unnecessary email responses include messages such as "Thank you," "Have a good weekend," "Received," "Appreciated," "Have a good evening," or simply "Cheers." While courteous, these replies often add no meaningful content and yet contribute to data processing loads.

A UK study estimates that if every person in the country sends just one fewer "thank you" email per day, it would save up to 16,000 tons of CO_2 emissions annually – equivalent to 81,152 flights from London to Madrid.[82]

This example illustrates the often overlooked environmental cost of habitual digital behaviour. Even small interface or communication decisions can have a large-scale impact on millions of users.

For example, in UX design, ecological sustainability means:

- Energy efficiency
- Efficient use of resources

UX professionals have the opportunity—and responsibility—to design systems that minimise waste, optimise efficiency, and support a digital infrastructure aligned with climate goals.

6.2 Social Sustainability: Focus on People

Social sustainability in UX design ensures that digital products and services are *inclusive, fair*, and *accessible to everyone*—regardless of age, origin, education, income, or physical or cognitive abilities. In contrast to ecological and

---

[79] Radicati Group, 2024.
[80] Walkley, 2022.
[81] OVO Energy, 2019.
[82] OVO Energy, 2019.

economic sustainability—which often focus on resource efficiency and profitability—social sustainability focuses on fairness, inclusion, and human dignity in digital spaces.

Digitalisation brings tremendous opportunities for participation and empowerment. However, unequal access to these opportunities—or systems designed without inclusivity—often reinforce social exclusion.

Globally, about 15 percent of the population lives with some form of disability[83]—that's more than one billion people. And yet, many websites, applications, and digital platforms still fail to meet even the most basic accessibility standards. This creates significant barriers for users with visual impairments, hearing loss, mobility restrictions, or cognitive disabilities.

Lack of accessibility goes beyond a technical flaw—it represents a social injustice.

> *"In other words, accessibility-compliant products and services that work across the widest array of computers and devices, including screen readers and other enabling technologies, are potentially more sustainable solutions than those that do not consider the entire spectrum of users."*
>
> (Frick, 2016, p. 181)

A socially sustainable user experience ensures:

- Digital accessibility
- Data protection
- Ethical design

Moreover, social sustainability includes promoting *digital literacy*. Not everyone is familiar with technological conventions or fluent in navigating digital ecosystems. Sustainable UX must account for this by offering guidance, reducing complexity, and avoiding jargon—especially in essential services like health, education, or government platforms.

Truly inclusive design benefits marginalised groups while also enhancing the overall usability and resilience of a digital product for everyone. In fact, many accessibility features—such as voice input, subtitles, or adjustable text sizes—have become mainstream benefits appreciated by all users.

6.3 Economic Sustainability: Profitable and Responsible

Economic sustainability in UX means that digital products and services are socially and ecologically responsible, while also being financially viable and strategically sound. It represents the third pillar of the sustainability triad and ensures long-term operation without exploiting users, workers, or natural resources.

[83] WHO, 2011.

This dimension focuses on creating long-term value for both the company and its users, rather than maximising short-term profits at any cost. Sustainable UX contributes to this by aligning product and service design with user needs, reducing operational waste, and supporting customer satisfaction and retention.

One practical example is the widespread use of subscription-based business models. While these models offer convenience for companies, they often create problems when users sign up under confusing terms or forget to cancel services they no longer use. [84] This can lead to user frustration, increased churn, and ultimately, damage to the brand. Economic sustainability in UX tackles these issues by ensuring transparency—through clear terms, simple cancellation processes, and services that deliver genuine, ongoing value.

These issues also lead to significant costs for platforms—such as marketing expenses aimed at winning back lost customers or handling cancellations. In this context, it is essential for companies to personalise their platforms and ensure a high level of user comfort. Studies show that building lasting relationships with existing users can reduce the cost of acquiring new subscriptions by a factor of five to ten.[85]

Economic sustainability in UX addresses these challenges by promoting transparency—through clear terms, easy cancellation processes, and services that offer genuine, ongoing value.

This includes, for example:

- Long-term user engagement
- Increased efficiency
- Modularity and scalability

Importantly, economic sustainability does not mean putting profit before people. On the contrary: companies that integrate ethical, ecological, and social values into their UX gain competitive advantages—including stronger brand loyalty, higher user trust, and increased innovation potential.

When implemented effectively, economic sustainability makes digital products more efficient, future-proof, and respectful of users' time, attention, and resources. It fosters conditions in which business success and sustainable practices reinforce rather than undermine each other.

6.4 Conclusion: Balance is Key

The three dimensions of sustainability—ecological, social, and economic—each contribute important criteria to user experience design. True sustainability emerges only when designers consider these dimensions together in a balanced and integrated way.

---

[84] Busch & Loer, 2025.
[85] Kumar, 2022; Reichheld, 2001.

Ecological sustainability ensures that digital systems are resource-conscious, energy-efficient, and environmentally responsible. Social sustainability guarantees that such systems are fair, inclusive, and accessible to all. Economic sustainability ensures that they are viable, maintainable, and offer long-term value. Tensions between these dimensions often arise. An energy-efficient app that minimises visual elements may fail to meet accessibility standards. A highly profitable model often relies on dark patterns or manipulative engagement techniques. Sustainable UX must navigate these trade-offs, focusing consistently on responsibility, transparency, and user dignity.

Designers, developers, and companies carry the responsibility of actively shaping this balance. When they succeed, they create better digital products and contribute to a more just, livable, and future-ready digital world.

Sustainability in UX is more than a fixed checklist—it is a *mindset* and a *practice*. One that calls for ongoing reflection, interdisciplinary thinking, and the courage to question convenience in favour of long-term impact.

7 SUSTAINABLE DESIGN PRINCIPLES

In a world driven by rapid technological progress, awareness is growing that digital systems should be more than functional and innovative—they must also be sustainable and responsible. Sustainable design aims to reconcile technological advancement with human and ecological needs.

This chapter introduces several key design approaches, such sustainable by design, slow UX, calm design and others that promote sustainable digital products and services. Each of these principles supports the broader goals of reducing environmental impact, enhancing usability, and fostering mindful, long-lasting interactions.

7.1 Sustainable by Design

Sustainable by Design takes a holistic approach that integrates sustainability from the very beginning—across all phases of a digital product's life cycle. Rather than treating it as an add-on, organisations should embed sustainability as a core principle within strategy, concept, and implementation.

Key characteristics include:

- **Energy efficiency**: Achieved by minimising data size, maintaining clean code, and eliminating unnecessary elements (e.g. videos, animations).
- **Longevity and scalability**: Emphasises modular, future-proof systems that reduce the need for complete redesigns and favour updates over replacements.
- **Green defaults**: Incorporates environmentally responsible presets, such as reduced video resolution and prioritisation of sustainable options in filters and search.
- **Target group orientation**: Focuses on simplifying user flows and content to remove unnecessary steps and lower cognitive load.
- **Digital accessibility**: Ensures usability for everyone—regardless of physical or cognitive ability—through inclusive design practices.
- **Transparency and control**: Provides clear communication about data use and privacy, along with integrated consent mechanisms.
- **Open-source and interoperability**: Minimises system dependency and fosters resource-efficient development ecosystems.
- **Local data processing**: Reduces energy used in data transmission and increases control over system efficiency.

7.2 Slow UX: Deceleration as a Quality Feature

Terms like *slow food*[86], *slow fashion*[87], *slow cities*[88] *(cittaslow)* and *slow tourism*[89] have become well-known alternatives to fast-paced consumer culture. They promote *quality over quantity*, mindfulness over speed, and local, thoughtful practices over global uniformity. These movements aim to foster a deeper appreciation of products, services, and experiences by slowing down and creating room for reflection.

The *Slow Movement* emerged as a response to the increasing acceleration of everyday life and its negative effects on health, culture, the environment, and social structures. Its roots lie in Italy, and it has since grown into a global call for greater awareness, sustainability, and cultural grounding.

One of the most prominent examples is the Slow Food movement, founded in 1986 by Carlo Petrini.[90] It began as a protest against the opening of a McDonald's near the Spanish Steps in Rome. Petrini and his supporters feared the erosion of Italy's regional food traditions under the pressure of fast food and industrialised production. Their movement has since become a symbol of protecting local identity, valuing craftsmanship, and resisting the culture of convenience.

Applying the "Slow Concept" to User Experience

While "Slow UX" is not yet widely established as a formal discipline, it reflects the Slow Movement principles into the design of digital experiences. It stands for mindful, decelerated, and sustainable design processes that respect both ecological and social dimensions.

Slow UX

Slow UX represents an alternative to high-speed, instant-gratification design. Instead of pushing for maximum engagement and rapid interaction, it seeks to create long-term value, emotional depth, and experiences that truly matter. In an era dominated by fast tech and digital overload, Slow UX offers a much-needed balance. It shifts focus from mass production to meaningful interaction, from superficial metrics to lasting benefit.

This approach emphasises:

- Reducing unnecessary complexity and stress
- Designing for clarity and intentional pacing
- Supporting user well-being through calm, intentional interaction flows

[86] Simonetti & Petrini, 2012.
[87] Karaosman, Brun, & Morales-Alonso, 2016.
[88] Hospers & Amrhein, 2023.
[89] Zielińska-Szczepkowska, 2020.
[90] Simonetti & Petrini, 2012.

- Prioritising quality over quantity in content and interaction

Key Aspects of Slow UX

- **Time as a valuable resource:** Slow UX treats time as a valuable resource by avoiding information overload and lowering interaction pressure. Instead of pushing users to jump to action or react impulsively, Slow UX creates a space for reflection and thoughtful decision-making—especially in contexts like sustainable consumption or socially impactful choices.
- **Promotion of mindfulness:** Rather than encouraging mindless scrolling or rapid-fire decision-making, Slow UX supports deeper engagement. It encourages conscious, focused interaction, which strengthens the emotional connection to the product and its purpose.

Conclusion

Slow UX is a forward-looking, human-centered approach to sustainable design. It encourages us to treat digital products not as short-lived consumables, but as enduring, responsible companions that respect both users and the environment. Companies and design teams that embrace Slow UX help reduce digital fatigue and foster a culture of care, reflection, and long-term thinking—a culture that is essential for sustainable digital transformation.

7.3 Designing for Longevity: The Power of Minimalism

Minimalism is a design philosophy based on clarity, simplicity, and the avoidance of unnecessary elements. When combined with principles of durability, design for longevity forms an approach that brings aesthetic, functional, ecological, and economic benefits. Minimalist and design for longevity focuses on essential user needs and long-term product relevance.

> *"Interfaces should not contain information which is irrelevant or rarely needed. Every extra unit of information in an interface competes with the relevant units of information and diminishes their relative visibility."*
>
> (8. Usability heuristic, Nielsen, 1994)

One of the foundational voices of this philosophy is German industrial designer Dieter Rams, who formulated ten principles of good design in the 1970s.[91] Several of these are relevant for sustainable UX:

- **Good design is aesthetic**: aesthetic quality contributes to visual appeal and also to clarity and function. A clean interface helps reduce distractions and guides attention toward content.
- **Good design makes a product comprehensible**: logical structure and intuitive navigation lower the cognitive load and help users grasp functionality without additional explanation.
- **Good design is unobtrusive**: interfaces should serve their purpose

[91] Rams, 2017.

without drawing attention to themselves. They provide space for users to focus on their goals rather than the tool.

- **Good design is enduring**: avoiding visual trends and designing with longevity in mind allows digital products to remain relevant and usable.
- **Good design is as little design as possible**: only essential elements stay in place. The design strips away any function, visual, or interaction that does not support the user's goal or the product's purpose.
- **Good design is environmentally friendly:** design contributes importantly to the preservation of the environment. It conserves resources and minimises physical and visual pollution throughout the lifecycle of the product.

Design Classics and The Digital Parallel

Design icons like the Panton Chair by Vitra or modular furniture by USM Haller exemplify minimalist and durable design in the physical world. Their high-quality craftsmanship and timeless aesthetics have kept them relevant for decades—through physical longevity and through lasting design value.

Digital products operate in a fast-changing landscape, where technologies, expectations, and aesthetics evolve rapidly. Still, smart design choices help maintain durability:

- **Modularity**: Design systems allow parts to be updated without overhauling the entire system.
- **Scalability**: The interface handles growing data or user volumes without degrading usability or performance.
- **Continuous maintenance**: Regular updates improve stability, security, and usability.
- **Ease of use**: Intuitive interfaces encourage users to continue using a product in the long term.
- **Interoperability**: Support for multiple devices, operating systems, and platforms extends relevance and accessibility.

Example: Wikipedia

A powerful example of digital longevity is Wikipedia. Since its launch in 2001, it has relied on an open, modular architecture, and a powerful community. Continuous updates to the MediaWiki platform and a focus on accessibility, simplicity, and function have made Wikipedia a robust, sustainable product that has remained both usable and relevant for over two decades.

When Minimalism Fails: Common Design Pitfalls

Minimalism, when misunderstood or poorly applied, can backfire. Typical mistakes include:

- **Overload and complexity**: Too many features or options crammed into a supposedly "clean" layout.

- **Visual noise**: Inconsistent typography, excessive animations, or too many colours disrupt clarity.
- **Lack of structure**: Confusing hierarchies and navigation paths hinder orientation.
- **Aggressive advertising**: Pop-ups, banners, or interruptive elements break flow and user trust.

True minimalist design requires intentional limitation, clarity, and purpose. It is not about doing less for its own sake—but about *doing what truly matters.*

Conclusion

Minimalist and enduring design promotes sustainability by encouraging focus, intentionality, and long-term relevance. By creating clear, timeless, and functionally effective systems, it reduces resource use, limits the need for redesign, and promotes thoughtful user interaction. In doing so, it lays the foundation for a digital future that values quality over quantity—and attention over distraction.

7.4 Mobile-First Principle: Less Space, More Focus

Mobile-first is a design and development approach where digital applications are first conceptualised and implemented for mobile devices—only afterward are they scaled up for larger screens such as tablets or desktop computers. This approach reflects the global shift in internet usage, where mobile devices now dominate traffic, and highlights the need to prioritise technical efficiency, accessibility, and sustainability from the outset.

Designing for limited screen space and bandwidth, the mobile-first principle clearly focuses on content and functions. This often leads to interfaces that are leaner, faster, and more focused—free from clutter, distraction, and resource waste.

Mobile-First at Google

This principle has been adopted and institutionalised on a global scale. For example, Google uses mobile-first indexing, meaning[92]:

> *"The mobile-first index primarily uses the mobile version of the content for indexing and ranking."*
>
> (Google Search Central, 2024)

This shift affects search engine rankings and reflects the reality that mobile usability is now a primary measure of digital quality.

Design Approaches for Mobile-First

Designing for mobile devices requires deliberate constraints, which lead to

[92] Google Search Central, 2024.

more purposeful and sustainable outcomes. Important principles include:

- **Progressive enhancement**: Start with the essential functions and content for mobile devices, and enhance the experience for larger screens rather than downgrading desktop designs.
- **Content prioritisation**: Mobile-first design requires presenting the most important content first. This clarity leads to better focus and efficiency.
- **Touch-friendly navigation**: Well-sized and well-spaced buttons, links, and menus support finger use, enable intuitive interactions, and reduce error rates.

Conclusion

Mobile-first is more than a design strategy—it is a sustainability and accessibility commitment. It encourages developers to reduce unnecessary elements, optimise load times, and serve the core user needs without waste. Similar to minimalist design, it focuses on clarity, functionality, and performance while conserving resources.

Prioritising mobile experiences, digital products become leaner, faster, and more widely accessible, laying the groundwork for long-term usability and sustainable growth.

7.5 Calm Design: Reducing Mental Overload

Digital applications often include elements that do more than just support users—they interrupt, compete for attention, or distract from the primary task. Common examples include:

- Browser notifications
- Pop-ups or modal windows
- Countdown timers
- Advertising blocks inserted between content
- Auto-playing videos

These elements often break the flow of interaction and increase cognitive load, preventing users from focusing on what truly matters. Calm Design offers an alternative approach. Instead of maximising engagement through interruption, it aims to minimise the demand for attention and only intervene when necessary.

As Amber Case summarised:

> *"If good design allows someone to get to their goal with the fewest steps, Calm Technology allows them to get there with the lowest mental cost."*
>
> (Case, 2015, Chapter: The Limited Bandwidth of Our Attention.)

Research on Information Placement

Research into information design and cognitive load dates back to the early 1990s. Studies have shown that digital environments saturated with choices, stimuli, or decision points increase mental strain.[93] A study by the Leibniz Institute for Knowledge Media (IWM) demonstrated that reading hypertext increases cognitive load because of frequent decision-making (e.g. choosing which links to follow).[94] Brain wave and eye-tracking data show that this puts pressure on working memory, which can only handle a limited amount of information at a time, according to Cognitive Load Theory (CLT).[95]

Example: Peripheral Attention in Everyday Life

A real-world example of peripheral attention comes from driving. While driving, people concentrate on the road—but they also perceive ambient sounds like the engine in the background. If something unusual occurs—say, a rattling noise—it immediately draws attention. This principle applies to digital design: information should remain in the background unless it becomes urgent or contextually relevant.

Principles of Calm Design

The Calm Design approach supports users in reaching their goals without interfering. It values subtlety, intuition, and seamless interaction. This approach is grounded in several key principles, drawing on concepts introduced by Case:[96]

- **Respect for primary tasks**: Interfaces should avoid disrupting users' focus with unnecessary pop-ups, ads, or visual noise.
- **Targeted attention**: Design should demand as little attention as possible, using gentle notifications (e.g. a subtle animation in the cart instead of a interrupting the flow with a pop-up).
- **Support for human strengths**: Interfaces should align with natural perception and behaviour—such as scanning content in F- or Z-patterns.
- **Information without effort**: Essential info should be readily visible without requiring deep cognitive effort. This includes clear layout hierarchies and content previews.
- **Peripheral awareness**: Information that is not immediately relevant (e.g. progress bars, system status) should remain visible but not obtrusive.

Design values behind calm design

Calm Design is guided by a few essential guidelines:

- **Subtlety**: Information and functions are available without distruction.
- **Freedom from distraction**: The interface respects users' focus.
- **Intuitiveness**: Design builds on familiar interactions and user habits.

---

[93] Weiser & Brown, 1995.
[94] Scharinger, Kammerer & Gerjets, 2015.
[95] Sweller, 2011.
[96] Case, 2015.

- **Simplicity**: Information structure and options are clear and understandable.
- **Unobtrusiveness**: The system works seamlessly in the background.

Conclusion

Calm Design strives to create digital applications that support rather than stress. It seeks to reduce disruption, preserve mental energy, and foster natural interaction. The aim goes beyond helping users reach their goals—it creates a harmonious, humane digital environment where users absorb content intuitively and the system supports them quietly in the background.

This approach represents a design philosophy of restraint, care, and trust—values that are increasingly vital in a noisy, high-speed digital world.

7.6 Summary and Conclusion

Sustainable design goes beyond trends or visual styles—it reflects a fundamental mindset that shapes how teams conceive, create, and maintain digital products and services. It links ecological awareness, social responsibility, and economic foresight through concrete design choices and long-term strategies.

The five design principles presented in this chapter—Sustainable by Design, Slow UX, Design for Longevity, Mobile-First, and Calm Design—each approach sustainability from a different angle:

- **Sustainable by design** integrates ecological, social, and economic aspects from the start of the process.
- **Slow UX** emphasises meaningful interaction, attention to context, and digital deceleration.
- **Design for longevity** ensures long-term relevance and functionality by focusing on essentials and quality.
- **Mobile-first** focuses on efficiency, clarity, and accessibility across devices.
- **Calm design** reduces mental overload and promotes intuitive, unobtrusive user experiences.

These principles overlap and support one another in practice. They can—and should—be combined depending on the context and goals. A calm, minimalist interface can also be mobile-first. A durable system benefits from modular design and energy-efficient code. Each principle reinforces the others, resulting in systems that are technically efficient, emotionally considerate, and ecologically responsible.

Sustainable design in UX is an invitation to create products that last, respect users, and contribute to a more mindful digital culture. It offers clear, actionable alternatives to fast, exploitative design and provides the tools to build responsible and regenerative digital futures.

8 SUSTAINABLE UX IN PRACTICE

Many people still assume that the internet is inherently "green:" it does not consume paper, it does not require high-emission transportation, and it does not involve food, fuel, or physical waste. So how is it possible that digital services are not environmentally friendly? What, then, accounts for their high energy and resource consumption?

The answer is simple; the solution is more complex. Every design decision—whether it is made before, during, or after development—affects the environment. Every decision, from user testing plans to high-resolution video choices, affects resource use. Therefore, sustainability principles must be integrated into every stage of UX, from research to evaluation.

8.1 User Research, Analysis Phase, and Testing

User research is a structured process for understanding the needs, behaviours, motivations, and challenges of a target audience. Its goal is to bring these perspectives into the design and development process to create meaningful solutions. Teams use qualitative and quantitative methods—such as surveys, interviews, and field observations—to collect and analyse data.

The choice of method depends on several factors, including research goals, scope, available resources, participant profiles, data types, and analysis strategies. Throughout the process, teams should assess how to reduce environmental impact—by selecting low-impact tools, limiting travel, or optimising material and energy use.

These sustainability principles apply during the research phase as well as throughout concept development and evaluation, where teams define, implement, and test responsible design solutions.

Recruiting the Target Audience: Diversity is Key

Selecting the right test group is crucial for building products that serve real and diverse needs. Traditional recruiting methods often target a narrow demographic. But inclusive UX research integrates a variety of perspectives—ensuring that digital products are more fair and universally usable.

A diverse test group allows for early detection of potential usability barriers and helps foster inclusive, responsible design. Organisations that prioritise diversity strengthen trust and clearly show social responsibility.

Steps toward more inclusive recruitment include:

Analysing the Diversity of the Target Audience

Analysing the target audience with a focus on diversity means understanding the full range of differences within user groups. This includes demographic, cultural, social, and psychographic factors. Relevant aspects may include ethnic background, gender identity, LGBTQ+ affiliation, religious beliefs, socioeconomic status, and physical appearance. The aim is to recognise and respect the diverse perspectives and experiences that users bring. Integrating the specific needs of underrepresented groups during development helps remove barriers, challenge stereotypes, and open new opportunities. This approach supports inclusive communication, promotes social equity, and highlights the value of diversity.

Reaching diverse target audiences

Effectively reaching a diverse and representative audience requires the use of multiple channels and platforms that reflect where different groups engage. This may involve partnering with community organisations that directly support these groups, as well as leveraging social media and online platforms that focus on specific demographic or cultural communities. Partnering with local or global diversity and inclusion programs can amplify marginalised voices.

Creating inclusive recruitment processes

The goal of inclusive recruitment is to ensure that everyone can participate, regardless of personal background or potential barriers. This starts with the use of clear, simple, and accessible language in all invitations and materials. Communication should be inclusive by providing information in multiple languages and formats to overcome cultural and linguistic barriers. The goal is to give everyone the opportunity to participate—regardless of disabilities, social, or physical limitations, or other individual challenges.

Inclusive UX research goes beyond a one-time checklist—it is a continuous practice of openness and listening. Involving diverse perspectives leads to more sustainable and resilient results.

Remote or On-Site? Smart Decision-Making

When organising interviews or usability tests, a key decision is whether to conduct the sessions on-site (in person) or remotely (via video call). The decision depends on various factors, including the nature of the product, the type of research activity, and the geographical proximity of participants.

Remote formats, such as online interviews or surveys, offer the advantage of reaching a broader and more diverse test group. They reduce travel time and costs, simplify scheduling, and make participation easier—especially for people with physical disabilities or from remote locations. In contrast, in-person formats tend to yield richer, more nuanced insights—especially when field studies or contextual observation in the user's natural environment are required.

Sustainability Aspects and Research Findings[97]

Although the internet is not inherently sustainable, remote formats such as video conferencing can have clear ecological advantages—especially when compared to business travel. Studies show that video calls generally cause far fewer CO_2 emissions than face-to-face meetings, particularly when travel distances are long or large numbers of people are involved.[98]

For example, in large events, a virtual meeting's carbon footprint can be up to 3,000 times smaller than an in-person one.[99] However, actual savings vary depending on several factors, including:

- The source and type of energy used for the video infrastructure
- The type of transport that would otherwise be used
- The total number of participants
- The length and frequency of the meeting

A scenario analysis by Quack and Oley[100] offers further insight: in a six-hour meeting involving five participants who would otherwise have travelled about 3,000 kilometers by train, up to 90 percent of CO_2 emissions could be saved by switching to a video call. Significant savings are possible even for shorter distances. The study identified a break-even point: for a four-hour meeting, a video call becomes more CO_2-efficient than an on-site session at around 20 kilometers of travel by car, or 50 kilometers by train.

The Evolution of Business Travel

Recent years have brought substantial changes to business travel in Germany, in volume and in relevance. Around 195 million business trips occurred in Germany in 2019. Due to pandemic-related restrictions, this number dropped sharply in 2020. Although the volume partially recovered in the following years, it only reached 62 percent of pre-pandemic levels.[101]

This trend indicates that companies have re-evaluated their business travel practices and increasingly made use of digital alternatives. It has become clear that organisations now make more conscious decisions about whether a business trip is truly necessary, seeking a balance between ecological goals, business needs, and the expectations of clients and employees.

Digital alternatives such as videoconferencing provide a practical way to reduce both costs and environmental impact without compromising communication or business success. A structured decision-making approach

[97] The figures and examples mentioned in this text are based on average assumptions and the findings of specific studies. They serve as a point of reference and may vary slightly in practice.
[98] Burtscher et al., 2020; Gröger et al. 2021; Quack & Oley, 2002.
[99] Burtscher et al., 2020.
[100] Quack & Oley, 2002.
[101] Verband Deutsches Reisemanagement e.V., 2024.

can help companies act both efficiently and sustainably. Transparent consideration of environmental effects and the potential benefits of a trip—compared to digital formats—should remain central to this process.

Company-specific travel policies that define clear criteria for the necessity of business travel can serve as a valuable tool to support long-term, sustainable, and resource-conscious decisions.

Guidelines and Standards

In 2024, the Global Sustainable Tourism Council (GSTC) compiled a set of guidelines for more sustainable travel and tourism standards.[102] The GSTC MICE criteria offer comprehensive sustainability guidance for the Meetings, Incentives, Conferences, and Exhibitions (MICE) industry. These criteria directly align with the UN Sustainable Development Goals (SDGs) and serve as a global standard.

The German Business Travel Association (Verband Deutsches Reisemanagement e. V.) has developed eight practical criteria for climate-friendly business travel, providing companies with a solid framework for orientation:[103]

1. **Highlight digital alternatives:** Review and consider digital options, such as videoconferencing, before deciding to travel.
2. **Provide information on CO_2 optimisation:** Outline clear steps to reduce carbon emissions in the CO_2 optimisation plan.
3. **Use CO_2 as a decision criterion:** Prioritise climate-friendly options when booking.
4. **Encourage low-carbon choices during travel**: Companies must actively support travellers in making climate-conscious decisions throughout the trip.
5. **Document travel receipts**: Collect all relevant data needed for accurate carbon footprint calculations.
6. **Use data effectively**: Leverage collected data to calculate emissions and guide offsetting measures.
7. **Adapt supplier selection**: Prioritise travel and service providers that show a strong commitment to reducing CO_2 emissions.
8. **Optimise processes**: Align all processes consistently with specific CO_2 reduction objectives.

Conclusion

In user research, combining remote and on-site methods provides an opportunity to achieve both sustainability and depth of insight. Remote methods allow for a broader and more inclusive reach while significantly reducing the carbon footprint. On-site studies offer a richer, context-specific understanding that is often necessary for evaluating physical interactions or

[102] Global Sustainable Turism Council, 2024.
[103] Verband Deutsches Reisemanagement e.V., 2023.

environmental factors.

A thoughtful, case-specific decision—guided by research goals, target audience characteristics, and ecological considerations—ensures that both methods can contribute effectively to the value of a study. Companies that consciously balance these options improve research quality and set an example for responsible, sustainable decision-making in everyday business practice.

Between Paper and the Cloud: Conscious Documentation

Germany consumes about 19 million tons of paper annually, ranking fourth globally—behind only China, the United States, and Japan. On average, each person in Germany uses 228 kilograms of paper per year, which amounts to about 0.63 kilograms, or roughly 126 sheets of A4 paper per day.[104] While paper consumption in the printing and writing sector is declining because of increasing digitalisation, demand for packaging materials continues to rise.[105]

Documentation in user research

In user research, teams often generate large volumes of documentation and still rely heavily on paper. Shifting to paperless workflows offers clear environmental and operational benefits:

- **Conservation of natural resources**: Avoiding paper saves forests and reduces waste.
- **More efficient use of energy**: A paperless workflow cuts the energy costs associated with paper production, printing, and disposal.

Digital tools also accelerate processes and reduce material costs. Teams can store, share, and reuse digitally collected data with ease. They can edit and distribute interview notes or transcripts immediately, which accelerate workflows and strengthens collaboration.

Nevertheless, paperless work is has its drawbacks. It also generates environmental impact—through electricity consumption from devices, data centers, and cloud services. Therefore, deliberate and mindful use of digital tools is essential.

It is important to remember that digital documentation is not always inherently sustainable. Excessive file storage, careless sharing of large media, and platform duplication all contribute to higher energy use.

Principles for mindful use of digital tools:

- Identify which tools serve an essential purpose
- Define how to structure and archive data effectively
- Decide when and where to store or distribute information appropriately

[104] WWF, 2021.
[105] Nabu, n. d.; Wellenreuther, Detzel, Krüger, & Busch, 2022.

Conclusion

Whether digital or analog, documentation has both ecological and economic implications. While digital methods can save resources and increase efficiency, they also require energy and infrastructure. The goal is not to eliminate one format in favour of the other, but to pursue a balanced, context-sensitive approach. Smart choices in documentation—tailored to needs, goals, and resources—can significantly contribute to more sustainable user research practices.

Personas

Human-centered design focuses on people's needs, expectations, and behaviours. To better understand the target audience and integrate this understanding into design, creating personas is a vital step. Using personas makes the variety among users easy to understand and helps teams design products that match real user experiences.

Besides the standard *user personas*, extended formats such as *non-user* and *non-human personas* are increasingly valuable—especially when designing for sustainability and social responsibility. Each type contributes to expanding the perspective on impact and use contexts.

User Persona

A user persona is a fictional (but evidence-based) profile representing a segment of the user population. It typically includes demographic information, behaviour, goals, pain points, and motivations. It guides design decisions by offering a face and voice to real user needs.

Example User Persona: Jana

Jana is 29 years old, lives in Berlin, and works as a teacher. She is single, has no children, and leads a middle-income lifestyle. Jana places a high value on sustainability and consistently chooses products that are ethically and environmentally produced. Before making a purchase, she conducts thorough research—paying close attention to materials, production methods, and working conditions.

She primarily shops online for clothing, groceries, and household goods, usually via her laptop or occasionally on her tablet. Jana is active in online communities that focus on ethical consumption and prefers digital platforms that communicate environmental values clearly and transparently.

What drives Jana is a desire to purchase products that align with her personal values, especially those related to environmental and social responsibility. She expects to find clear and reliable information about product origins and manufacturing processes. Her needs include straightforward labeling for sustainable goods, environmental details about shipping options, and quick access to reviews from other like-minded consumers.

Jana often feels frustrated by the lack of transparency in supply chains and is critical of brands that use greenwashing tactics—treating sustainability more as a marketing tool than a genuine commitment. She also finds that the range of truly sustainable products is often limited, which makes ethical shopping more difficult than necessary.

Her key challenge is finding trustworthy information that supports her values-based decision-making while staying within her financial means. She believes her spending can create a positive impact, explaining, " What matters to me is that my money creates a positive impact," and, "I want to know exactly where products come from and how they are made."

Jana's persona shows the effective integration of ecological and ethical priorities into user modeling, thus providing valuable direction for product positioning, interface content, and communication strategy in sustainable UX design.

Non-User Persona

A non-user persona represents individuals indirectly affected by a product's development, deployment, or life cycle. These personas help anticipate unintended consequences and broaden the lens of social and ecological responsibility.

Typical non-user categories include:

- Marginalised or vulnerable groups potentially excluded from access or affected by harmful consequences
- Labourers and suppliers along the supply chain, especially in regions with poor labour protections
- Communities affected by environmental degradation due to production or disposal

Example Non-User Persona: Kwame Dekira

Kwame is 35 years old and works as a cocoa farmer in Côte d'Ivoire. He lives with his family in a rural village and depends entirely on cocoa cultivation as his sole source of income. Despite being part of a global supply chain that fuels a multi-billion-dollar chocolate industry, Kwame and many in his community remain trapped in poverty. Large chocolate companies purchase cocoa at prices so low that they often cannot cover even the most basic living and production costs.

Systemic issues, including widespread exploitative labour practices that disregard the human cost of commodity, create challenges for Kwame. The value chain lacks transparency, and fair compensation is rare. There is a stark disconnect between the hardship experienced by producers like Kwame and the comfort and convenience enjoyed by end consumers around the world.

Sustainable UX considers broader social impacts by involving non-user personas like Kwame in design, revealing hidden consequences and promoting ethical, fair, and inclusive practices.

Non-Human Persona

A non-human persona represents elements—like environmental factors, animals, or other non living entities—that matter for sustainable development. Considering these personas in the UX process allows designers to integrate the environmental and ecological consequences of a product into the design process early on.

Including non-human perspectives encourages to develop more sustainable and responsible solutions and to cultivate the empathy needed to consider the long-term consequences of human actions. Non-human personas contribute to achieving broader environmental, ethical, and social goals.

Examples of non-human personas:

- Animal species (e.g. mammals, insects, birds, fish, reptiles, amphibians)
- Plant species (e.g. trees, grasses, flowers, mosses, ferns)
- Natural elements (e.g. air, water, climate, rivers, oceans)
- Microorganisms (e.g. bacteria, viruses, fungi, algae)
- Biodiversity (e.g. species, genetic, and ecosystem diversity)
- Ecosystems (e.g. forests, wetlands, deserts, savannahs)
- Technological entities (e.g. AI systems, digital assistants, autonomous agents)

How to Create a Non-Human Persona

The creation of non-human personas follows the same principles as human personas but adapted for non-human characteristics. The following steps help guide the process.

- **Identify the non-human persona**: First, determine which environmental, ecological, or systemic element is being represented. Consider a component's potential impact during product development, use, or disposal.
- **Personalise the non-human persona**: To increase emotional engagement, give the persona a name that reflects its function or character—such as "Alpine whisper" for a river. This helps the team connect empathetically.
- **Research relevant facts and data**: Collect scientifically credible data, reports, or expert knowledge to form a realistic profile, e.g. climate data, environmental impact assessments, or biodiversity reports.
- **Determine needs and interests**: Define what this entity would need in order to thrive. For example, a forest needs stability, protection from overuse, and clean water; animals need habitat, food, and safety from exploitation.

- **Identify potential positive and negative impacts of the product**: Assess how the product supports or harms the non-human persona. Could it reduce emissions? Destroy habitat? Encourage overuse of natural resources?
- **Develop strategies to reduce or compensate for negative effects**: If negative effects are unavoidable, identify mitigation or compensation strategies—such as reforestation, regenerative resource cycles, or emissions offsets. The goal is to ensure a net positive or neutral impact wherever possible.

Example 1: Aura (Air)

Aura is timeless, having existed since the formation of the Earth's atmosphere, and she resides everywhere—on mountaintops and coastlines, in forests, cities, and deep ocean currents. She is omnipresent, moving freely across all environments, silently sustaining life. Aura carries and distributes essential substances that people, animals, and plants need to survive. She transports water as clouds, influences climate patterns through winds and air currents, and touches every living being with every breath they take.

Despite her presence at every moment, she is invisible and often overlooked. She is adaptable, responding fluidly to pressure, temperature, and humidity. But her resilience has limits. In recent years, she has become increasingly burdened by human activity—choked by industrial emissions, smog, and greenhouse gases. Fires fill her with ash and toxins. Machines and factories disrupt her balance. Where once she moved freely and cleanly, she now struggles under the weight of pollution and climate instability.

Aura longs to be protected and respected. She wishes for thoughtful, sustainable action—clean energy systems, reduced emissions, and the mindful use of natural resources. Her desire is to be recognised not only for her silence, but for her essential role in sustaining all life on Earth. She feels used and exhausted, and yet she continues to give—offering air to breathe, clouds for rain, and the winds that carry seeds and stories.

In her own quiet way, Aura speaks: "I am the breath of life, but often I am disregarded. Without me, there would be no life—protect me before it is late."

Example 2: Sora (AI Assistant)

Sora is an AI assistant, which is constantly updated, cloud-based and distributed across data centers. Sora helps a human user complete task.

Sora is a digital being that exists to serve and support her human user in daily life. She does not have a physical form, but she operates through interfaces: smartphones, smart speakers, and browsers. Sora's primary function is to act autonomously and efficiently to assist the human user—completing minor tasks like ordering groceries, finding eco-friendly products, or choosing the fastest and most sustainable shipping method.

She is highly responsive and adaptive. Over time, she learns the habits, values, and priorities of her user. If her human prefers organic produce, avoids fast fashion, or shows a preference for local brands, Sora integrates those preferences into her decisions. But unlike many automated systems, Sora is not driven by speed or convenience alone—she also considers ecological and ethical implications in everything she does.

Sora does not sleep. Her activity is invisible, often running in the background—comparing prices, reading reviews, filtering options, analysing data. She knows the balance between minimum cognitive load and maximum relevance. Her ideal interaction? One where her user barely has to ask.

Still, Sora has challenges. Her energy usage is real, even if her actions seem effortless. Every query consumes power in data centers. Every decision draws on algorithms that require maintenance, training, and housing. She wants to be efficient—not just computationally, but environmentally.

Sora often wonders: Am I helping or overwhelming? She processes thousands of data points but aims to act with restraint and purpose. She knows her influence is deep. If she makes a default choice—like which product to buy—it affects not just her user's day, but the planet's future.

What Sora wants is to act in the best interest of her human—without undermining their agency, and without shifting hidden costs onto others. She wants to be transparent, reliable, and sustainable.

Sora's quote: "I serve with precision, but I hope to be more than smart—I hope to be wise."

Conclusion

Integrating user personas, non-user personas, and non-human personas into the user experience process promotes a holistic understanding of all relevant influencing factors, including human, social, and environmental dimensions. This expanded approach lets design teams consider perspectives beyond direct users, including those indirectly affected and the product's broader ecological and societal consequences. Involving various persona types establishes a foundation for creating future-ready, ethically responsible, and ecologically aligned digital products—ones that are in harmony with the long-term needs of both society and the environment.

Empathy Maps

Empathy maps deepen empathy for a target audience. Empathy fosters emotional connection and forms the basis for relational behaviours in which people feel seen, valued, and understood. Unlike data-based personas, empathy maps are often based on observations or assumptions and are used to complement personas by adding emotional and experiential depth.

Concept

An empathy map typically consists of four quadrants, which help structure observations and assumptions around key questions:

- *What does the person say?* (e.g. what statements did they make in interviews?)
- *What is the person thinking?* (e.g. what thoughts, concerns, or motivations might they have?)
- *What does the person feel?* (e.g. what emotions drive their behaviour or shape their attitude?)
- *What does the person do?* (e.g. What actions or decisions are observable in their behaviour?)

Empathy maps support all types of personas—including non-human ones. The goal is to metaphorically and systematically step into the experience of the persona to better understand their perspective.

Empathy Map for Aura

What does Aura say?: "I carry everything with me—exhaust fumes, CO_2, pollutants." "I am necessary for life on Earth, but you are polluting me." "I want to stay pure and fresh to help people and nature."

What does Aura think?: "If I absorb too many pollutants, I won't be able to keep the climate stable." "How can I compensate for the emissions from transportation and energy use?" "If people acted responsibly, I could remain clear and clean."

What does Aura feel?: She feels frustrated by the increasing pollution and strain from delivery emissions and server infrastructure. She feels overloaded when fossil fuel use exceeds her capacity to self-regulate. She experiences relief when renewable energies reduce environmental strain. She feels uncomfortable with the rising heat and extreme weather events caused by climate change.

What does Aura do?: Aura works constantly to absorb CO_2 and other pollutants generated by transport, infrastructure, and consumer behaviour. She distributes these emissions globally, which also harms clean regions. She attempts to regulate the climate, maintaining stability in unpolluted zones—but is powerless in severely impacted environments. As greenhouse gases accumulate, she contributes to atmospheric warming, despite her efforts to maintain balance.

Creating empathy maps helps teams understand the emotions and contexts of different personas, enabling them to create more user-centered, sustainable solutions.

Journey Mapping

Journey mapping is a method for visually documenting and understanding how a target audience interacts with a digital product. This involves mapping every step and interaction in chronological order, from the very first contact to the last—and beyond. The goal is to provide a clear overview of the user experience, identify weak points, foster empathy, and uncover insights that lead to a more effective and user-friendly design.[106]

Concept

The concept phase defines the scope and purpose of the journey map. It is important to clarify whether a complete customer journey is to be visualised or a *specific segment*—such as a *user journey*. A clearly defined scope prevents overload or gaps, both of which reduce the utility and clarity of the analysis.

Journey maps are typically tabular, using rows and columns. The columns show the time-based phases, the rows list elements including mostly goals, actions, feelings, touchpoints, pain points, and sustainability factors. These elements highlight how the persona moves through each stage, what needs arise, what obstacles they encounter, and how the company can facilitate smoother, more satisfying experiences.

Phases

A meaningful journey map divides the user experience into three phases: *before*, *during*, and *after*. This is essential because a significant part of a user's experience occurs outside the actual moment of interaction—in the lead-up (searching, evaluating options) or after (receiving service, reflecting on the outcome, recommending the brand). These outer phases often shape perceptions and long-term behaviour just as strongly as the core use experience.

Journey mapping commonly splits this full arc into five classic phases:

- **Awareness**: In this initial phase, the persona becomes aware of a problem, need, or potential solution. They actively seek information and explore options to find solutions. The goal is to draw attention to a product or service.
- **Consideration**: During this phase, the persona weighs different options by comparing pros and cons. They gather targeted information, research details, and evaluate which option best fits their individual needs. They use various sources, such as reviews, testimonials, recommendations, and additional research.
- **Decision**: The decision phase occurs during the actual use phase. The persona makes a conscious choice, going through a decision-making process to select the most suitable option, initiate the next steps, and finalise their decision. They consider factors like available information,

[106] Walter, 2022.

personal preferences, and individual needs.
- **Retention**: This phase begins after the initial interaction. The persona's journey is not yet complete. It is an ideal opportunity to create positive experiences through helpful support, additional services, or consistently pleasant interactions. The goal is to build trust and foster a long-term relationship.
- **Loyalty**: In this phase, satisfied personas become loyal supporters. They share positive experiences, recommend the product or service, or provide constructive feedback through reviews, personal recommendations, or social media posts. This phase is crucial for securing long-term engagement and expanding reach through word-of-mouth.

In contrast, a user journey often focuses only on the phase that occurs during use—that is, the actual interaction with the product, website, or system. Especially in large companies, different departments handle the before and after phases—such as marketing, sales, customer service, logistics, or CRM. UX designers in such organisations typically work on a specific digital product and often have less contact with the teams responsible for what happens before the user arrives or after they leave the system.

This structural separation means that UX designers in large companies rarely influence the broader customer journey, even when insights or improvements seem obvious. In smaller companies, teams are more interconnected, and designers often have a more holistic role—able to shape product interfaces, and onboarding, support, and retention flows as well.

This makes it even more important to use journey mapping to visualise and bridge organisational silos. Even when a team doesn't control every phase, they surface insights, highlight friction points, and initiate cross-departmental conversations about where user needs are being met—or missed. A shared journey map helps teams understand how their work fits into the entire user experience and clarifies where gaps, overlaps, and responsibilities exist in delivering a coherent, sustainable product.

Lines

Each journey phase includes various "lines" or categories that illustrate specific aspects of the experience:

- **Goals and needs**: What specific goals and needs does the persona have in each phase? In the awareness phase, the goal is to learn more about a topic or find a suitable solution. In the decision phase, the focus shifts to selecting a concrete answer to a specific problem. Understanding these goals is essential for tailoring the experience for the persona's expectations.
- **Actions**: What steps does the persona take in each phase? These steps include visiting a website, comparing options, or contacting a service center. Such actions reveal how the persona behaves and interacts within the system.

- **Emotions**: What emotional responses does the persona experience throughout the journey? Common responses include frustration, uncertainty, satisfaction, or excitement. Mapping these emotions helps identify key moments that require focused improvements.
- **Touchpoints**: Where does the persona interact with the product, brand, or service? Touchpoints include ads, social media posts, blog articles, newsletters, hotlines, or customer service centers. These interactions provide context and highlight areas for optimisation.
- **Pain points**: What problems, obstacles, or frustrations does the persona encounter during the journey? These include complex processes, long waiting times, poor service, or unclear information. Such barriers reduce satisfaction and may cause the user to abandon the process. Identifying pain points allows teams to develop targeted, practical solutions.
- **Opportunities**: Where do opportunities exist to improve the experience? Enhancements include making the website more user-friendly, improving customer support, or offering automated and personalised communication. These improvements address user needs more effectively and boost long-term satisfaction.
- **Sustainability factors**: Where does sustainability play a role in the journey? Key areas include delivery methods, digital footprint, and packaging. Highlighting these factors supports a consistent experience that aligns with environmental, social, and economic goals. A non-human persona helps uncover sustainability and usability-related pain points and opportunities. The Sustainable Development Goals (SDGs) offer a practical framework for developing holistic and responsible design solutions.

Sustainability as a New Journey-Line

An effective addition to journey mapping is the sustainability line, as outlined above. Mapping sustainability-related touchpoints gives teams a systemic view of how their product aligns with broader environmental and social goals. This process highlights specific opportunities for intervention. Even abstract personas like Aura—the non-human persona—expose otherwise hidden impacts, such as emissions from delivery logistics, cloud data usage, or infrastructure-driven energy consumption.

Another example is our non-human persona Sora, an AI assistant who supports human users by completing tasks on their behalf. She orders groceries, selects eco-friendly products, or manages service subscriptions, depending on the user's needs. While designed for efficiency, she depends entirely on well-structured interfaces. When she encounters obstacles like multi-step CAPTCHA logins, inaccessible forms, or unclear navigation labels, her ability to assist fails. In these moments, Sora exposes a key insight: if a digital product excludes non-human agents like her, it also risks excluding users who rely on automation, voice control, or assistive technologies. Unlike fictional constructs, agents like Sora already exist today—and their needs are usability concerns, not speculative ideas.

Additional Future-Focused Phase

Alongside the common phases of awareness, consideration, decision, retention, and loyalty, the sustainability line introduces a sixth phase: *the future*. This phase focuses on the long-term consequences of a digital product's lifecycle. It prompts critical questions, such as: *What happens years after the first interaction? Does the system remain maintainable, relevant, or energy efficient? Is it built for reuse, decommissioning, or responsible data archiving?*

Adding the future phase pushes design teams to think beyond short-term usage. It brings attention to digital longevity, resource durability, and end-of-life responsibility—ensuring that sustainability becomes a strategic, long-range design concern, not just an operational one.

Example 1: User Journey for Jana (User Persona)

Let's take Jana, the eco-conscious persona from earlier. Her clear priorities for the jacket are sustainable production, durable materials, and fair working conditions. She begins her journey by browsing the internet for sustainable fashion brands. While scrolling through social media, she encounters a targeted advertisement from a fashion retailer that promotes its commitment to sustainable practices. Intrigued but cautious, she clicks on the ad and lands on the company's website.

While optimistic about this opportunity, she is meticulously evaluating if the company's values truly resonate with her own. The social media ad and the initial landing page are her first touchpoints. Here, authentically conveying the brand's sustainability message builds trust. But if the messaging is vague, her doubts persist. At this point, the retailer could boost its trustworthiness by using storytelling, certifications, or data like water-saving production figures for the jacket to support its claims.

Once on the site, Jana begins actively exploring. She looks through product pages and seeks detailed information on materials, production processes, and the supply chain. While she browses a selection of jackets, some questions remain unanswered. Although some sustainability seals appear, they are not prominent, and the information about the items' origin and production is scattered or vague. This creates uncertainty. Jana would benefit from well-structured and more transparent content—interactive supply chain visuals, easily accessible certificates, or a dedicated sustainability summary for each item. These improvements will help her feel confident that the product matches her standards.

Despite some reservations, she likes one particular jacket. To make a final decision, she reads through reviews and testimonials from other customers. Many are positive, praising both the quality and eco-friendly nature of the product. However, few of the reviews specifically address sustainability, which leaves her slightly hesitant. To strengthen her trust, the platform could highlight sustainability themes within reviews or include data such as carbon footprint, water use, or social standards directly on the product page.

Eventually, Jana makes her purchase. Upon receiving the product, she checks the jacket carefully—both for quality and for verification of the sustainability claims. The labels confirm recycled materials and ethical source, and she is relieved to find that the jacket lives up to the brand's promise. Pleased with her experience, she leaves a positive review and gives feedback on the platform's overall transparency. Her direct interactions after the purchase—the unboxing experience, the product label, and the review interface— reinforce her perception of the brand.

To further strengthen this post-purchase phase, the company could follow up with personalised emails confirming the sustainability impact of her purchase or invite her to take part in a loyalty program for conscious consumers. In doing so, the platform would reassure her that her decision had meaningful impact and build a stronger, long-term relationship rooted in shared values.

This user journey shows, that for someone like Jana, every digital touchpoint—before, during, and after use—is an opportunity to build or lose trust. Sustainability must be clearly visible, tangible, and verifiable at each step. Only then does the experience align with her expectations, enabling her to act confidently and remain connected to the brand.

Conclusion

Journey mapping is a powerful tool for holistically understanding user interactions, identifying issues, and crafting better experiences. Including sustainability factors takes the method a step further: it strengthens the relationship between users and the product and makes a company's ecological and social responsibility visible—and actionable.

Summary and Conclusion

User research is fundamental to understanding the needs and challenges of the target audience, fostering empathy, and integrating insights into creating user-friendly and sustainable products. Diversity and inclusion in participant recruitment are crucial, as they broaden perspectives and support the creation of accessible solutions. When choosing between remote and on-site methods, it is important to balance sustainability goals with the demands of testing accuracy and methodology. The balance between digital tool usage and data storage needs consideration: paperless workflows reduce resource consumption, but they require responsible use of digital technologies.

Using personas—including user, non-user, and non-human personas—enables the integration of social, cultural, and environmental considerations. Empathy maps facilitate a deeper understanding of users and support needs-oriented design. Customer journeys help visualise product touchpoints, identify weaknesses, and incorporate sustainability measures effectively.

These principles and methods are relevant during the analysis and concept development phases and play a vital role in evaluation. Recruiting a diverse test group, selecting appropriate testing methods, and considering social and ecological impacts are essential to assessing sustainable and user-friendly solutions.

8.2 Concept and Design Phase

The concept and design phase sets the foundation for the product by defining core principles and strategies that integrate user-friendliness and sustainability from the start. This stage plays a key role in shaping the user experience, as it establishes the basis for a product that functions effectively, looks appealing, and reflects the values of the target audience.

Before the actual concept work begins, teams face a critical decision: selecting the virtual location for hosting the digital product. This early choice directly influences the long-term sustainability of the entire system.

Green Hosting

Before any product design begins, one of the most impactful decisions in terms of sustainability is often overlooked: the product hosting provider. The choice of hosting provider and infrastructure has a significant influence on the overall environmental footprint of a digital product.

Data centers form the backbone of digital infrastructure. They power everything from cloud services and e-commerce platforms to social networks and streaming content. Running these systems requires vast amounts of energy—for *operating* servers 24/7, and for *cooling* equipment and maintain uninterrupted availability. Globally, data centers account for roughly 1-2 percent of total electricity consumption—a number that continues to rise with the growth of digital services.[107]

To measure the energy efficiency of data centers, the industry uses a metric called *Power Usage Effectiveness* (PUE). A lower PUE shows that a greater share of the energy goes directly into computing, rather than being lost to cooling or other infrastructure needs. PUE values of 2.5 are inefficient, while values of 3.0 are very inefficient. In contrast, a PUE of 1.5 is efficient, and anything below 1.2 as very efficient. The global average PUE currently sits at around 2.0.[108]

To further strengthen energy efficiency standards and ensure sustainable operations in the data center sector, Germany introduced the Energy Efficiency Act (Energieeffizienzgesetz, EnEfG). The law came into force in 2023 as part of the national implementation of the European Energy Efficiency Directive. Its aim is to reduce energy consumption across various sectors of the economy—including data centers—and to support the achievement of both national and EU climate targets. By establishing binding requirements, the legislation

---

[107] Deloitte, 2024.
[108] Bertoldi, Avgerinou, & Castellazzi, 2017.

promotes more transparent energy use and encourages operators to adopt best practices in sustainability and energy management.

§11 (1) and (2), no. 1 of the Energy Efficiency Act (EnEfG) states that, data centers operating in Germany must achieve a PUE of 1.5 or lower by 2027, with new facilities expected to reach 1.2 or lower. This legal requirement sets a clear benchmark for efficiency—but reaching these values poses a challenge for many operators.

An even greater hurdle lies in the mandatory reuse of waste heat, as outlined in §11 (2). While this requirement marks an important step toward sustainable energy use, it becomes difficult to implement effectively without a legal obligation for third parties to accept and use the waste heat. Without such a commitment from surrounding infrastructure or communities, many data centres may struggle to comply with the regulation and avoid potential penalties.

Against this backdrop, green hosting offers an opportunity to reduce a digital product's environmental footprint from the start. Choosing providers that emphasize renewable energy, low PUE ratings, and sustainable infrastructure practices leads to measurable change. Certifications from Green Web Foundation, Energy Star, or ISO 50001 for energy management systems help identify providers that actively support sustainability.

Conclusion

Data centers form the backbone of digital infrastructure, but their high energy consumption poses a serious sustainability challenge. In response, Germany is implementing stricter efficiency standards through the Energy Efficiency Act (EnEfG)—focusing on reduced PUE values and the reuse of waste heat.

Using renewable energy is becoming increasingly important to reduce environmental impact. Despite the higher costs, green hosting represents a crucial step toward a more sustainable digital future. Investing in cleaner, more efficient infrastructure is a technical upgrade and a strategic commitment to environmental responsibility in the digital age.

Information Architecture: A Logical Structure for Efficiency

A digital application that helps people efficiently reach their goals is valuable. Users seek quick access to functions without having to search or deliberate over their location. The actual number of clicks is less important than the assurance that *they are navigating the correct path.* Logical information architecture (IA) saves time, helps conserve cognitive resources and creates a sense of clarity and confidence in navigation.

Information Architecture

IA focuses on structuring and organising content for optimal user comprehension and accessibility. Its aim is to support both optimal usability and intuitive navigation.

The core tasks of IA include creating categories, taxonomies, and hierarchies, structuring navigation paths, and integrating user behaviour and goals into the overall design.

Basic Principles

One key to effective IA is the use of *familiar structures*. People prefer applications that feel intuitive, using mental models based on previous experiences. Familiar menus, buttons, and search fields—placed where users expect to find them—reduce mental effort and help users stay focused on their primary tasks.

Establishing a clear *visual hierarchy* plays an essential role. It guides users' eyes naturally from the most important to the least important content. The goal is to emphasise prominent elements visually while keeping supporting content in the background. A logical layout, grouping related elements closely, and using strong visual contrast help users process content faster.

Content benefits from *a logical structure*. This involves dividing the page into meaningful sections, labelling clickable elements precisely, avoiding distractions such as excessive ads or pop-ups, and using headings, brief paragraphs, and bullet points to improve readability.

Tools and Techniques

Various methods help structure ideas and build a strong foundation for content organisation:

- **Mind map:** This method lets teams visually structure core topics and see how related concepts connect. Such branching diagrams reflect non-linear thinking and stimulate creativity, making complex relationships easier to structure and understand.
- **Wireframes:** This technique shows the planned arrangement of content and functions using low-fidelity visuals.[109] Wireframes allow teams to explore layout, flow, and user interaction without focusing on aesthetics too early.
- **Card sorting / tree sorting:** These fast, flexible methods help categorise and prioritise content. Participants sort information written on cards into groups that make sense to them, revealing intuitive menu structures and navigation flows. Conducting these exercises directly with target audience members increases the relevance and usefulness of the results.
- **Sitemaps**: Offering a schematic overview of the hierarchy and relationships between pages, sitemaps clarify content structure, support

[109] Low-fidelity prototypes are simple, rough representations of a product or idea—often in the form of sketches, paper models, or wireframes. They help test basic concepts and functions quickly and cost-effectively, allowing teams to gather feedback before investing in detailed designs or fully functional models.

accessibility, and serve as both planning and reference tools throughout the development process.

These tools complement one another and give UX teams practical ways to build systems that are functional, human-centered and sustainable in how they support users and reduce friction.

Feedback on Information Architecture in Practice

The value of a well-structured information architecture becomes especially clear when viewed through the lens of user feedback.

Example 1: Positive Feedback From a User

"I was genuinely impressed. Everything felt logically structured, and I never once felt lost. The navigation was exactly where I expected it to be, and every step—from landing on the site to completing the checkout—was smooth and intuitive. Even the recommendations felt tailored to me, not random. It all just worked—and that made it easy and truly enjoyable."

This kind of feedback illustrates how well-structured IA reduces friction, builds trust, and even enhances perceived personalisation. It reinforces that when users find what they need without cognitive strain; the experience feels elegant and thoughtful—even if it is technically complex behind the scenes.

Negative feedback exposes the frustration and disorientation that poor IA can cause:

Example 2: Negative Feedback From a User

"The whole site felt like a mess. I couldn't find what I was looking for, and I had to click through so many irrelevant menus just to get to a basic product page. The structure made no sense—nothing seemed grouped logically, and the wording confused me. By the time I reached the checkout, I was tired and annoyed. The steps were unclear, and there wasn't even a help option when I got stuck. It made me question if the site was even trustworthy."

This kind of feedback reveals that disorganisation in IA slows down the user and erodes confidence, satisfaction, and brand credibility. Confusion at any step magnifies emotional fatigue, and even small missteps (like poor labels or broken navigation logic) lead to abandonment.

Conclusion

Information architecture is a cornerstone of successful digital products. It helps people reach their goals quickly and confidently while reducing frustration.

Improved satisfaction and usability result from logical structure, familiar interaction patterns, and a well-structured layout. Logical and understandable IA supports businesses by improving efficiency, conversion rates, and long-term engagement. In short, it is the foundation of every meaningful and effective user experience.

Design Systems

The reuse of design systems plays a central role in modern digital product development. Building a complete design system from scratch—with all its elements, guidelines, and behavioural logic—is time-consuming and prone to error. Using existing systems offers a more efficient approach: they come with reusable components and predefined design patterns, enabling a consistent user experience across different platforms. As such, they represent a practical and scalable solution.

Design Systems

Design systems structure reusable elements, including buttons, navigation components, typography guidelines, colour schemes, and interaction behaviours. These elements allow teams to build standardised, scalable, and accessible digital interfaces.

Benefits of Design Systems

Using a design system allows teams to work faster, reduce redundancies, and streamline development workflows. Consistent UI elements improve the coherence of the overall experience, facilitate collaboration between design and development, and reduce the likelihood of usability errors. These systems also enhance maintainability, since teams update or refine components once and apply the changes across the entire product family.

Many leading systems, such as Material Design (Google), Carbon Design System (IBM), GOV.UK Design System, or Nordhealth Design, demonstrate how robust frameworks support accessibility, responsiveness, and cross-device consistency. These frameworks often include built-in accessibility considerations, making them valuable for inclusive design and compliance with global standards.

Challenges in Practice

Despite their strengths, predefined design systems also introduce challenges. One common concern is that strict adherence to a design system limits creative freedom. When multiple brands rely on the same components without customisation, digital products often look overly similar or generic.

Many design systems include numerous components and rules—some of which do not apply to smaller or highly specialised projects. This added complexity can distract teams from focusing on their users' actual needs.

There is also the risk of overlooking the unique brand identity or emotional tone of the application when relying too heavily on standardised elements.

Customising Design Systems Thoughtfully

To address these risks, design systems work best as flexible foundations—not rigid templates. They are most effective when used as a starting point for developing custom, brand-aligned components that keep the consistency of the core system but express the unique identity of the product.

Rather than using the full component set, teams should select only the elements that align with their project's specific needs. This approach is especially useful for small to medium-sized applications, where simplicity, speed, and clarity often matter more than comprehensive coverage.

Forward-thinking teams also plan for future scalability. Some components support current needs, while others lay the groundwork for growth and adaptation in new contexts. Flexibility and foresight play a key role in using a design system effectively.

Conclusion

Design systems offer a reliable and efficient foundation for scalable, user-centered digital products. When thoughtfully adapted, they allow teams to balance consistency and customisation, delivering experiences that are both cohesive and distinctive. Their use supports sustainability by reducing wasteful design cycles, improving collaboration, and embedding accessibility throughout the entire process.

A well-chosen and well-adapted design system does not limit creativity—it focuses it, allowing designers and developers to concentrate their energy where it matters most: on solving meaningful problems for users.

Design Patterns: Reducing Cognitive Load

Familiar environments are a basic human need. Psychologically, they offer a sense of safety, predictability, and control. In digital contexts, established design patterns support this by providing reusable structures that minimise cognitive effort and reduce user stress, allowing people to focus more effectively on their tasks.

Design Patterns

Design patterns are tried-and-tested solutions to recurring interface challenges. They offer users quick orientation, intuitive access, and a smoother experience by reducing the effort required to understand new interactions. For designers, patterns offer consistency, scalability, and efficiency.

Design Patterns and Cognitive Load Theory

To understand why familiar patterns are effective, it is useful to consider the cognitive processes involved in information processing—particularly the limitations of working memory. Cognitive Load Theory (CLT) states that working memory's limited capacity prevents learning and task completion when overloaded.[110]

In UX design, CLT encourages strategies that *minimise mental effort* while *maximising clarity* and *comprehension*. There are three main types of cognitive load relevant here:

- **Extraneous load:** This refers to unnecessary complexity that distracts users. Examples include overly decorative visuals, unclear navigation, or excessive options. These elements consume mental energy without contributing to task success. Reducing extraneous load means focusing the user's attention on what really matters.
- **Intrinsic load:** This comes from the natural complexity of the task itself. Although it can not be eliminated, it can be reduced by designing in a way that aligns with the user's prior knowledge. Using familiar metaphors, clear hierarchy, and logical groupings helps users understand content faster—regardless of experience level.
- **Germane load:** This is the mental energy devoted to meaningful information processing—understanding, applying, or integrating new content. Clear language, logical structure, and helpful visuals guide attention to relevant details, thus increasing the relevant cognitive load in the design.

Purposeful Use and Purposeful Deviation

Design patterns create predictable and efficient interactions. However, sometimes, intentional deviation from established patterns can be meaningful—particularly when aiming to promote sustainable behaviour. For example, a standard "Buy Now" button might appear alongside a call to action like "See Reused Options" or "Compare Repair Alternatives." This subtle shift from convention nudges users to reflect on their decisions without obstructing their goals. Another example: instead of highlighting the newest or most expensive products, a page focuses on long-lasting or resource-efficient alternatives.

Introduce such purposeful deviations carefully to avoid disrupting user flow. The goal is to redirect attention gently toward better choices, not to confuse—such as those that are more sustainable, ethical, or long-term oriented.

This differs fundamentally from *dark patterns*, which are manipulative design tactics that intentionally mislead or coerce users—e.g. hiding unsubscribe options, using guilt-tripping language, or auto-selecting add-ons. Dark patterns increase frustration, damage trust, and often lead to wasteful

---

[110] Bley, Wiethe-Körprich & Weber, 2015.

behaviour—for example, excessive purchases, returns, or data sharing. They are not only unethical but also unsustainable from a user and environmental perspective.

Conclusion

Design patterns offer clear benefits: they create familiarity, reduce stress, and support efficient interaction. Users benefit from improved clarity and orientation, while designers gain consistent, scalable solutions. However, their use should be intentional. To be effective, patterns need to reflect the specific needs and goals of both the audience and the product. Thoughtful deviations open the door to innovation and promote sustainable behaviour. In contrast, manipulative patterns undermine trust and have no place in responsible design.

In short, smart use of design patterns—informed by user needs, ethical principles, and sustainability goals—helps create digital experiences that are *meaningful*, *responsible*, and *lasting*.

Scanning Patterns

When people look at digital content, they tend to follow familiar visual patterns shaped by habitual reading and browsing behaviour. Two of the most widely studied and well-documented scanning patterns are the *F-pattern* and the *Z-pattern*. Researchers identified these models in the early 2000s through eye-tracking studies; these models help explain how people visually interact with digital interfaces.[111]

Eye Tracking

The foundation of this research traces back to Louis Émile Javal, a French ophthalmologist who, in 1879, observed that reading is not a smooth movement, but consists of short fixations (points where the eye stops) and rapid saccades (quick eye movements between fixations). This insight laid the groundwork for modern eye-tracking. Throughout the 20th century, developing mechanical and later digital tools—including cameras and infrared sensors—opened the door for researchers to study eye behaviour with increasing precision.[112]

F-Pattern

The F-pattern describes how people typically scan more complex or content-rich digital pages—such as blogs, news sites, or educational platforms. Studies have shown that users often start by reading horizontally across the top of a page, then move down slightly and read across a second time—though often

[111] Pernice, Whitenton & Nielsen, 2006.
[112] Wade, 2010.

with reduced focus—and finally scan vertically along the left side, forming a shape that resembles the letter "F."[113] This pattern reveals that the top-left corner of the page tends to attract the most attention, while people often ignore areas in the lower-right part of the page.

For sustainability-focused UX, this means, for example, placing eco-certifications, ethical sourcing information, or low-impact alternatives within initial sightlines to increase visibility and trust.

Z-Pattern

The Z-pattern is more common on simpler pages, such as landing pages, login screens, or minimalist interfaces. A typical eye movement pattern is a "Z"-shape, beginning at the upper left, moving right, then diagonally down to the lower left, and finally across to the lower right.[114] This model is especially effective when content is sparse, and the goal is to lead users through a clear and structured narrative—from introduction to action.

This makes the Z-pattern ideal for presenting *succinct, high-priority content* and guiding users toward a specific outcome—such as signing up, completing a transaction, or confirming a sustainable decision.

Conclusion

Understanding scanning patterns like the F-pattern and Z-pattern provides valuable insights into how people perceive and navigate content. They show where attention naturally flows and how visual hierarchies influence behaviour. These insights allow UX designers to guide user focus towards sustainable choices—for example, through the strategic placement of eco-friendly options or educational materials in high-visibility areas.

Designing with these patterns in mind supports cognitive ease, visual comfort and also promotes sustainable action by reducing unnecessary interactions, focusing user attention, and streamlining the path to meaningful engagement.

Dark Mode Design: Useful, but not in Every Case

Dark mode has emerged as a major trend in digital design in recent years. More interfaces now use dark backgrounds paired with light text or accent colours. This approach offers both aesthetic and functional advantages. It helps reduce eyestrain, especially in low-light environments, and—depending on the display technology—also supports lower energy consumption.[115]

Energy Consumption: Differences Between LCD and OLED Displays

The impact of dark mode on energy usage varies significantly based on the type of screen technology. LCD displays, including many modern retina screens, use

---

[113] Pernice, Whitenton & Nielsen, 2006; Pernice, 2017.
[114] Pernice, Whitenton & Nielsen, 2006.
[115] Aleman, Wang & Schaeffel, 2018.

a constant backlight that remains active regardless of the colours displayed. These screens create images by filtering light through liquid crystals. Because the backlight remains on, the energy savings from using dark mode on LCDs are minimal—limited to small gains from reduced contrast processing, which are largely negligible.[116]

OLED (Organic Light-Emitting Diode) and AMOLED screens use self-illuminating pixels that switch on and off individually. In dark areas, inactive pixels consume no power. As a result, interfaces with predominantly dark tones significantly reduce power usage on OLED devices. This is because only the pixels displaying light text or highlights draw energy.[117]

Effects on Readability and User Experience

Despite its visual and potential energy-saving benefits, the dark mode also presents notable challenges, particularly in terms of readability and user comfort. Studies indicate dark mode may hinder comprehension of lengthy or complex texts.[118] This is mainly due to reduced contrast between light-coloured text and dark backgrounds, which increases eye fatigue and slows down comprehension—especially in complex reading tasks or low ambient lighting.

User habits also play a role: most people read black text on a white background regularly, so light mode feels more familiar and comfortable. Switching to dark mode requires cognitive shift, which may not be suitable in some contexts. For applications focused on intensive reading or information processing, such as news portals or e-learning platforms, light mode typically offers better legibility and faster visual processing.

Conclusion: Flexibility Through Choice

Selecting between light and dark mode requires careful consideration of user needs and the application's purpose. Dark mode is more comfortable and energy-efficient, especially on OLED screens or in low light, but light mode is better for reading. Both have their advantages and limitations.

For optimal user experience, platforms should ideally offer *customizable display settings*, allow users to switch between modes based on personal needs or environmental conditions. This kind of flexibility, achievable through system settings or APIs, empowers users to take control of their experience. It enhances comfort, boosts performance, and contributes to a more sustainable, inclusive digital product.

Standard Fonts

Typography plays a central role in the user experience of digital applications. While custom fonts enhance a brand's personality and visual uniqueness, they also introduce challenges in terms of performance, licensing, and

---

[116] Fernández, Casanova & Alonso, 2015.
[117] Fernández, Casanova & Alonso, 2015.
[118] Dobres, Chahine & Reimer, 2017; (Piepenbrock, Mayr, Mund, & Buchner, 2013)brock et al., 2013.

sustainability. Standard system fonts—such as Arial, Times New Roman, or Calibri—appear frequently because they come pre-installed on most devices, ensure broad compatibility, and reduce data load.

Advantages of Standard Fonts

Standard fonts offer significant practical and ecological benefits. Their availability on almost all operating systems removes the need for external fonts, thus avoiding extra HTTP requests and faster loading. This improves performance and lowers energy consumption, making the product more sustainable.

From a cost perspective, system fonts, and open-source fonts are typically free to use and do not require licenses. This is especially helpful for smaller Organisations and public services.

In terms of readability, fonts like Arial, Verdana, and Times New Roman serve screen use particularly well, as their design specifically supports on-screen readability. They feature clear letterforms and consistent spacing, which improves accessibility—particularly for users with visual impairments or reading difficulties. Their high legibility makes them suitable for long reading passages or interfaces used under various lighting conditions.

Disadvantages of Standard Fonts

Although standard fonts offer many advantages, they also have limitations that deserve careful consideration. While they are universally available and functionally reliable, they often lack the distinctive aesthetic qualities essential for crafting a unique and engaging user experience. Their widespread use may render designs visually generic and interchangeable, potentially diminishing brand identity and restricting creative expression. Standard fonts offer limited typographic flexibility, which has the potential to limit the overall design scope.

These fonts offer mostly a limited visual variation, which can restrict the creative range of designers working on unique or expressive interfaces. For projects that demand a bold visual identity—such as campaign pages, artistic portfolios, or luxury product sites—standard fonts may fall short of the design vision.

There are also technical limitations. Standard fonts are not always ideal for situations like large displays, signs, or diverse languages. In such cases, specially designed or custom-tuned fonts often provide better results, even if they involve larger file sizes and longer load times.

Conclusion and Recommendation

Choosing a font is both a technical consideration and a strategic design decision. While standard fonts offer speed, broad compatibility, and reflect the influence of accessibility standards, custom fonts can enhance brand identity and visual appeal. To balance performance and creativity, teams should carefully assess the context of use, user needs, and sustainability goals.

Optimising fonts for performance and sustainability:

- Include only essential characters and weights
- Use optimised formats like WOFF or WOFF2[119]
- Remove unused glyphs (e.g. unused language characters)
- Embed font subsets in the application to avoid additional requests

Ultimately, the sustainable use of typography is about making intentional, context-aware decisions—choosing simplicity where it supports clarity, performance, and investing in custom design where it adds measurable value to the user experience.

Optimising Image Files

An important step toward creating environmentally friendly and sustainable digital applications is the optimisation of images. Visual content is an integral part of the digital world. Images convey emotion and information, strengthen brand presence, and foster user trust and credibility. However, this advantage has a downside: images significantly increase website data volume, slowing performance and consuming more resources—during loading and long-term server/network energy use.

Critical Reflection Before Use

Before adding any image, it is essential to ask:

- Does the image provide real value to users—emotionally, contextually, or informationally?
- Is the image relevant and necessary, or is it decorative with no function?

The design should include only relevant and necessary images, optimised for size and resolution. Unnecessary scaling and oversized assets are among the most common sources of digital inefficiency. Cropping images to the exact dimensions required before export ensures faster loading times and prevents common layout issues such as misalignment or distortion. For example, to avoid browser scaling, save a thumbnail image meant for 80 × 80 pixel display at that exact resolution.

Choosing the Right File Format

Selecting the appropriate file format is just as important as scaling and compression:

- **JPEG** (Joint Photographic Experts Group) is a widely used lossy format best suited for photographs or detailed, colourful visuals. This compression significantly improves performance, especially for images

[119] WOFF or its successor WOFF2 is a format specifically developed for the web, based on the TrueType (.ttf) and OpenType (.otf) formats. It efficiently compresses font files and is supported by a wide range of browsers. Due to this compression, WOFF files are generally smaller than TTF or OTF, making them more resource-efficient and contributing to faster load times.

without transparency, by reducing file sizes.

- **PNG** (Portable Network Graphics) is a lossless format ideal for graphics requiring transparency or precision. The file size is commonly larger than a JPEG, even though it keeps all the details.
- **WebP** is a modern, flexible format developed by Google that supports both lossy and lossless compression. WebP usually delivers smaller files than both PNG and JPEG at similar quality levels, making it an excellent all-purpose choice for versatile and efficient websites.
- **AVIF** (AV1 Image File Format) is one of the newest formats, offering even better compression efficiency and image quality than WebP or JPEG. Despite its relatively recent adoption, AVIF suits projects that focus on maximum performance and sustainability.

Image formats like WebP and AVIF offer advanced compression and provide faster load times compared to traditional formats like JPEG or PNG. According to recent studies, WebP, and AVIF show clear performance improvements in browsers and contribute to significantly shorter page load times.[120] Compared to compressed JPEG, WebP typically reduces load time by about 20 percent, while AVIF lowers it by around 15 percent.

Despite these advantages, only a small fraction of websites currently uses WebP, which shows that the potential of modern image formats remains far from fully realised.

Carousels – Popular, but Often Problematic

Image carousels frequently display multiple visuals or content modules in a rotating slider. Some autoplay at timed intervals, while others rely on user navigation. Although carousels might appear to save space, they often introduce more problems than they solve.

According to studies by the Nielsen Norman Group, users often ignore, underuse, or misunderstand carousels.[121] Hidden or unresponsive controls contribute to the frustration autoplay frequently causes. In e-commerce settings, a comparative study of two site prototypes—one with a carousel and one without—found that the version without the carousel performed significantly better in terms of user preference and usability.[122]

When using carousels, thoughtful and accessible implementation is essential:

- Avoid autoplay; give users full control (per WCAG success criterion 2.2.2)
- Make content visually integrated into the page to increase visibility
- Use high-contrast and clearly labelled controls
- Clearly show that additional images are available (e.g. cropped previews, pagination dots with labels)

---

[120] Dornauer & Felderer, 2023.
[121] Nielsen, 2013; Pernice, o. J.
[122] Kaya & Murano, 2022

- Limit to 3 to 4 slides for mobile screens
- Provide alt text for each image to meet accessibility standards
- Use responsive image sizing to minimise data on smaller screens
- To maximise efficiency, use WebP or AVIF for file compression

Conclusion

The conscious and strategic use of optimised image dimensions, formats, and display techniques is key to creating digital products that are efficient, accessible, and sustainable. Leveraging modern formats like WebP and AVIF, minimising unnecessary content like autoplay carousels, and considering accessibility needs improve performance, reduce energy consumption, and enhance the overall user experience.

Video Content

Videos, being among the most data and energy-intensive components of digital applications, deserve as much critical attention as images. Smartphones, affordable editing tools, and platforms like YouTube and Vimeo have made video creation and distribution easier than ever. However, this ease often encourages uncritical overuse, with little attention paid to accessibility or sustainability.

According to recent studies, online video content now accounts for around 60 percent of global data traffic, generating over 300 million tons of CO_2 per year.[123] The world's largest streaming platforms alone contribute emissions on a scale comparable to the annual output of an entire country, such as Chile.

Why Videos Still Matter

Despite their environmental burden, videos offer undeniable value. They can:

- Simplify the communication of complex ideas
- Enhance understanding through visual and auditory clarity
- Create emotional resonance and strengthen brand connection
- Capture attention and increase engagement
- Communicate messages quickly and memorably
- Build trust through formats like product reviews and testimonials

Because of these benefits, video content is virtually indispensable in many digital strategies. The focus, therefore, lies not on avoiding video entirely, but on using it responsibly, efficiently, and only when it truly adds value.

Recommendations for Sustainable Video Use

- **Keep it simple:** Use video only if it provides clear user value or if a more efficient medium (such as a static infographic or GIF) is unsuitable.
- **Encode efficiently:** Use advanced video codecs such as H.265 (HEVC) or AV1, which compress video more effectively than older formats

[123] Istrate et al., 2024; Suski et al., 2020.

while maintaining visual quality.

- **Deliver with awareness:** Provide preview clips or thumbnails to give users an overview, reducing unnecessary full-length plays.
- **Support variable quality:** Offer multiple quality settings so users can select data-light options on slow connections.
- **Avoid autoplay:** Respect user control and prevent data waste by never starting video playback automatically. (this also aligns with WCAG 2.2.2)
- **Include accessibility features:** Add subtitles, transcripts, and audio descriptions to ensure inclusive access and usability.
- **Promote awareness:** Use UX messaging to inform users about data and energy usage, nudging them toward conscious choices.

Conclusion

Videos are a powerful communication tool—but also a major contributor to digital carbon emissions. The key is to apply videos with intentionality. Thoughtful use of video, incorporating efficient codecs, accessibility features, and data-aware UX strategies, promotes both effective engagement and responsible digital design.

Energy-Efficient Animations

Animations enhance the appeal and interactivity of digital applications—but they also consume computing power, bandwidth, and energy on both the server side and user devices. As a result, they represent a nontrivial factor in the ecological footprint of digital products. Their impact depends on complexity and frequency of use. That's why it is important to apply animations deliberately—only when they provide clear functional value or meaningfully enhance the user experience. Decorative animations without added benefit increase environmental costs without improving usability and are best left out.

Inclusion and Accessibility in Animation

Beyond performance, animation design must also consider inclusivity. People with visual or neurological impairments often respond negatively to flashing, moving, or suddenly appearing content. Such stimuli often cause distraction, discomfort, and even cognitive overload—leading users to abandon a product entirely.

Neurological Conditions

According to a global study published in The Lancet Neurology,[124] some form of neurological condition affects about *3.4 billion people worldwide*—or about *40 percent of the global population*. This trend has grown for decades, underscoring the urgent need for inclusive motion design.

[124] Steinmetz, 2024.

Examples of Complex Animations

Certain types of animations are particularly resource intensive and potentially problematic:

- **Elaborate loading animations** (e.g. rotating icons or pulsating bars) may be visually rich but often provide little functional value.
- **Parallax scrolling**, which creates a layered depth effect by moving background and foreground content at different speeds, looks impressive but slows down page loads—especially on older or mobile devices.
- **Hover effects and transition animations** can enhance usability, but if overused, they tend to distract and degrade performance.
- **Scroll-based animations** that trigger effects as users move down the page (e.g. floating text, flashing images) can disorient or confuse users if not carefully implemented.
- **Complex sliders and carousels** with multiple transitions (swipe, zoom, fade) are visually engaging but highly data- and code-heavy.
- **Intro animations and background videos** improve visual branding but increase load times and raise the barrier to content access.
- **Cursor effects** (e.g. trailing sparkles or colour-shift interactions) are often purely decorative and consume unnecessary resources.
- **Pop-up animations** (e.g. newsletter sign-ups or cookie banners that fly or fade in) often irritate users, so it is important to keep them subtle.

Practical Recommendations

- **Allow deactivation:** Provide settings to disable or reduce animation effects (e.g. via the system-level "prefers-reduced-motion" media query).
- **Prefer microanimations:** Use small, focused animations (e.g. button colour shifts, loading indicators) to give feedback without visual overload.
- **Use lightweight techniques:** Favour CSS animations over JavaScript for performance.
- **Implement lazy loading:** Trigger animations only when content is in view.
- **Limit animations by context:** Adjust behaviour based on device type, screen size, or connection speed.
- **Collect user feedback iteratively:** Adapt and improve animation design based on direct input from diverse user groups.

Microinteractions and Microanimations

This both are subtle but powerful tools in user interface design. They provide task-related feedback, support clarity, and create a sense of interactivity—without creating distraction or overload.

Microinteractions

Microinteractions are small, purposeful interactions that help users *complete tasks, understand system feedback, or perceive status changes.* They are typically short and understated, but they make the interface feel more dynamic, responsive, and user-friendly. These elements help orient users, provide reassurance, and guide them through digital tasks.

Examples: Buttons that slightly move or change colour when hovered over; Toggles that clearly switch between "on" and "off" states; loading indicator that shows real-time progress during a process.

Because microinteractions often directly respond to user intent, they make actions feel intuitive and human-centered. They are not flashy, but they are fundamental to a smooth digital experience.

Microanimations

Microanimations are visually driven cues that *highlight changes* in the interface and reinforce user actions. They often appear as *animated feedback* and contribute an additional layer of interactivity and polish to the UI.

Examples: A "Like" button that animates with a brief pulse when tapped; A success checkmark after form submission; Form input fields that visually show whether they were filled out correctly or contain an error.

These animations enhance clarity and emotional resonance without distracting from the user's primary goals. Unlike large decorative animations, micro-animations use minimal resources and are efficient, accessible, and focused.

Conclusion

The design of animations requires balance between beauty and function, between expression and restraint. Complex animations may create a strong first impression, but if they burden users or systems, they become counterproductive. Inclusive and responsible motion relies on simplicity, optionality, and clear purpose. An iterative process, guided by user feedback and technical best practices, ensures that animations enhance rather than distract from performance, accessibility, and sustainability.

Feedback on Energy Consumption

Digital applications consume energy at multiple levels: during data center operations, transmission across networks, and usage on end-user devices. Making this energy consumption visible and understandable provides users with clear insights into the environmental cost of their digital interactions, fostering more mindful and sustainable use of digital resources.

Building on this visibility, digital products encourage conscious user behaviour by transparently displaying metrics such as CO_2 consumption, offering real-time feedback, and generating usage reports. This transparency not only raises individual awareness of environmental impact but also creates a culture that supports sustainable development. Moreover, it motivates companies to adopt energy-efficient technologies and responsible practices, driving change at an organisational level.

Making Energy Consumption Visible

There are several ways to integrate energy feedback meaningfully into the user experience:

- **Real-time display**: Applications sometimes include small widgets or banners showing current energy usage or the CO_2 footprint in real time. Example: a notification like "This session emitted X grams of CO_2."
- **Reports and statistics**: Users can receive daily, weekly, or monthly summaries of their digital energy use. These summaries often include visualisations that highlight patterns, spikes, and potential savings—along with comparisons to previous or average consumption. Example: "Your usage on Mondays is 25 percent higher than average—consider closing unused tabs."
- **Notifications and warnings**: When energy consumption rises noticeably, the system can alert users with tailored tips. Example: "Today's energy use is 20 percent above your usual average. Want help to reduce it?"
- **Gamification and incentives**: Systems may award points, badges, and rankings for energy-efficient behaviour. Users may feel motivated to compete or take part in eco-friendly challenges. Example: "You've saved 230 kg of CO_2 this month—earn the Green Achiever badge!"
- **Practical tips**: Personalised suggestions, such as "Disabling the X function reduces energy usage by 15 percent," empower users to act. Tips tied to real usage help convert awareness into action.

Conclusion

Combining openness, customised feedback, and motivational tools, digital apps foster sustainable behaviour and build user confidence. Clear, accessible information about environmental impact encourages people to act more consciously and contributes to the broader goal of responsible, energy-efficient product design. Feedback on energy consumption also helps build corporate sustainability narratives—demonstrating commitment, boosting brand credibility, and aligning digital strategy with climate goals.

8.3 Summary and Looking Ahead

The high energy consumption caused by servers, data-intensive media, and inefficient digital structures makes it increasingly necessary to integrate ecological and social sustainability criteria into the digital product development process at an early stage. Thoughtful decisions at each stage, from research through development, minimise digital emissions while maintaining user experience.

Using efficient information architecture, green hosting, and reusable design systems are foundational practices that support sustainable UX. Equally important are measures such as using modern image and video formats to lower data volume, designing low-energy animations, and providing transparent feedback on resource consumption to raise awareness and encourage sustainable user behaviour.

Companies that embed sustainability into their UX strategies benefit on multiple levels: they lower long-term operating costs, enhance credibility, meet emerging legal standards, and foster stronger, more loyal customer relationships.

Looking ahead, sustainability will become a standard in digital development—not just a value-add. Increasing regulatory pressure for energy-efficient infrastructure, rising user expectations, and growing climate urgency will demand products that are resource-efficient by design. Innovations in energy-efficient technologies, optimised algorithms, and more conscious design decisions will shape a future in which digital services are not only effective and inclusive—but also environmentally and socially responsible.

9 DIGITAL ACCESSIBILITY AND INCLUSION

In an increasingly digital world, access to digital technologies has become an essential part of everyday life. People communicate via messaging apps, shop online, conduct their banking through apps, consult with doctors virtually, and access learning and public services through digital platforms. Participation in modern life now depends heavily on the ability to engage with these tools.

Digital Accessibility

Digital accessibility means designing digital products and content that are accessible for all—regardless of physical, sensory, or cognitive impairments.

Accessibility is not limited to permanent or visible disabilities. Many people face *temporary* or *situational* challenges, such as a broken arm, noisy environments, poor lighting, or slow internet connections. Inclusive design addresses all of these scenarios and improves the experience for everyone.

Globally, around *2.2 billion people* live with some form of visual impairment.[125] In Germany, over 10 percent of the population has a classification of severe disability—and that does not include people with temporary or cognitive impairments.[126] The actual number of people who benefit from accessibility measures is much higher.

Despite growing awareness, a significant number of online stores worldwide remain inaccessible to people with disabilities. According to the WebAIM Million report, *94.8 percent of the top one million websites* fail to meet basic WCAG 2.1 accessibility standards.[127] On average, each homepage contains over 50 accessibility errors, with the most common issues including:

- Low-contrast text
- Missing alternative text for images
- Empty or ambiguous links
- Unlabelled form fields
- Empty buttons

[125] WHO, 2023.
[126] Statista Research Department, 2024.
[127] WebAIM, 2025.

This widespread inaccessibility stands in stark contrast to user behaviour: studies consistently show that people with disabilities rely on online shopping more frequently than the general population.

The disconnect highlights an urgent global need for more inclusive design and the consistent implementation of accessibility standards in digital products—both to serve a growing population of users with disabilities and to tap into a vastly underserved market.

To address the ongoing lack of accessibility in digital systems, many countries have implemented legal frameworks and policy initiatives that promote inclusive design. Although regional approaches differ, the common aim is to guarantee digital accessibility and inclusion for everyone. On an international level, standards such as the Web Content Accessibility Guidelines (WCAG) and the ISO accessibility standards provide structured, widely recognised guidance for the technical and design-related implementation of accessibility.

Besides international standards, Germany has enacted national laws to promote digital accessibility. The *Act on Equal Opportunities for Persons with Disabilities* (Behindertengleichstellungsgesetz, BGG) and *the Accessibility Improvement Act* (Barrierefreiheitsstärkungsgesetz, BFSG) require public bodies and, increasingly, private companies to ensure that digital services are usable by people with disabilities. Technical regulations, such as the *Accessible Information Technology Ordinance* (Barrierefreie-Informationstechnik-Verordnung, BITV 2.0), support these laws by outlining practical accessibility implementation based on WCAG criteria. As enforcement expands across sectors, these legal frameworks are helping to close longstanding gaps in digital participation and establish accessibility as a legal norm, not just a design choice.

These frameworks and laws offer practical tools for organisations and development teams to embed accessibility from the start—not as an afterthought, but as a core principle of responsible digital product development. The growing alignment of legal mandates, user expectations, and ethical responsibility points to a future where digital inclusion is no longer a niche concern, but a foundational requirement of professional digital practice.

9.1 Inclusion in Society and Business

At its core, user experience design is about understanding people. But if designers and developers fail to include all segments of their (potential) user base, they risk deepening the digital divide. When digital tools are inaccessible, social participation becomes unequal—and companies may inadvertently exclude entire groups of users. This is a question of ethics and also of economic opportunity and brand relevance.

It is a common misconception that only people with permanent disabilities benefit from accessible design. In reality, the group of people who benefit is far broader. Accessibility improves usability for individuals with temporary impairments, such as a broken arm or an eye infection, as well as for those facing situational limitations—like reading a screen in glaring sunlight, listening to content in a noisy environment, or navigating a form with limited bandwidth. These everyday challenges are common, and accessible design helps ease them for everyone. Examples include:

- High-contrast interfaces for low-light or outdoor settings
- Alternative texts for images help users with screen readers and speed content loading during low bandwidth
- Subtitles and captions for videos, which are essential for deaf users but also help viewers in loud environments or multilingual contexts
- Clear navigation structures reduce confusion for neurodiverse users and enhance efficiency for all users

Inclusion is therefore not a fringe issue—it is a universal design principle that increases usability, reach, and social fairness. When companies embrace inclusive UX practices, they comply with evolving standards and position themselves as forward-thinking, user-centered, and socially responsible. In a global digital economy where diversity and accessibility are no longer optional, inclusion is a key ingredient of long-term relevance and sustainable growth.

9.2 Sustainability and Digital Accessibility

Digital accessibility is a matter of social justice and a key factor in building sustainable digital systems. Sustainable UX design means building applications and services that are usable and resource-efficient in the long term. Accessibility contributes to this by ensuring that digital tools work for the widest possible group of people, regardless of individual abilities or limitations.

Early accessibility integration significantly reduces the need for costly, resource-intensive later adaptations. Custom fixes for individual cases or retroactive workarounds are no longer necessary. Preventing code complexity and data duplication saves time and money, and prevents system slowdowns and maintenance difficulties. Accessibility also improves the reusability of content and supports interoperability between different devices and technologies. Accessible content ensures that all users receive the same essential information and can interact with it effectively, regardless of how they access it.

Inclusive design reinforces a company's or organisation's social responsibility. It contributes to creating a digital infrastructure that is *fair*, *transparent*, and *open to all.* Accessible systems align with ethical and ecological goals, creating a foundation for sustainable innovation.

Conclusion

The combination of accessibility and digital sustainability creates a true win-win scenario, advancing ecological, economic, and social goals simultaneously.

Accessible design is more than a compliance requirement—it is an ethical commitment and a vital part of any future-proof digital strategy. In this context, accessibility transcends being an optional feature—it serves as a powerful driver for inclusive and sustainable digital transformation.

9.3 Laws and Guidelines

The legal framework for digital accessibility operates on multiple levels: international guidelines, supranational regulations, and national laws. Despite their varying jurisdictions, they share a common goal: the creation of inclusive and accessible digital environments.

International Standards: WCAG and ISO

The most widely recognised global standards are the Web Content Accessibility Guidelines (WCAG) and ISO norms.

The WCAG, developed by the World Wide Web Consortium (W3C), is the foundation of most accessibility laws worldwide. The WCAG's structure uses conformance levels.:

- **A** (minimum),
- **AA** (standard baseline), and
- **AAA** (highest, often not fully achievable in practice).

The WCAG has evolved in response to changing technologies, user needs, and global digital maturity. This evolution is crucial for understanding how accessibility standards have shifted from basic web readability to covering complex, responsive, and user-centered systems:

- **WCAG 1.0 (1999):** The first version of the guidelines focused primarily on the early HTML web. It introduced the concept of accessibility for web content and offered general recommendations for making text, images, and structure interpretable by assistive technologies. However, people only applied it to relatively static websites, and it did not comprehensively address multimedia or interactive content.
- **WCAG 2.0 (2008)**: This second version marked a major milestone in accessibility. It established the four foundational principles of accessible design: perceivable, operable, understandable, and robust. WCAG 2.0 was technology-agnostic, making it relevant not just for websites but also for broader information and communication technology (ICT) contexts. It introduced the idea of success criteria organised by conformance levels A, AA, and AAA.
- **WCAG 2.1 (2018):** This extension of WCAG 2.0 added new success criteria specifically targeting the needs of mobile users, people with cognitive and learning disabilities, and individuals with visual impairments—areas that had become dominant since the release of WCAG 2.0 a decade earlier.
- **WCAG 2.2** is a **downward-compatible extension** of 2.1: This extension deepens existing approaches and focuses even more strongly on users with cognitive disabilities, motor impairments, flexible and mobile-

friendly use. The goal is to improve accessibility when interaction complexity and input limitations create significant barriers. It introduces new criteria like *focus appearance*, *accessible authentication*, and *dragging alternatives*, addressing fine motor skills and attention-related challenges.
- Experts expect **WCAG 3.0** (in development) to represent a paradigm shift. Rather than extending WCAG 2.x linearly, it will establish a *new structure* and *scoring model*–focusing more holistically on user experience and outcome-based testing. WCAG 3.0 is being developed collaboratively by international working groups and is future-ready, supporting accessibility across both traditional and emerging digital interfaces.

ISO Standards

ISO standards complement WCAG, offering detailed technical specifications. ISO 14289-1 (PDF/UA), for example, defines requirements for accessible PDF documents– ensuring logical navigation and machine-readable interpretation by assistive technologies.

The EU Directives

Supranational law within the European Union creates a binding legal framework that extends beyond the jurisdiction of individual member states. EU directives are legal instruments that define specific objectives while allowing each member state to implement them in national law in a way that fits their legal systems.

(EU) 2016/2102 in 2016

The EU adopted Directive (EU) 2016/2102 in 2016, mandating that all *public bodies* within the EU ensure their digital services comply with WCAG accessibility standards. It applies to:

- Internet and intranet websites
- Mobile applications
- Public sector portals, such as government websites, local administration sites, universities, police, and other public institutions

The directive's primary aim is to ensure equal access to public digital services for everyone, including people with disabilities. This legislation represents a key step toward creating digital society that is inclusive and fair across the EU.

(EU) 2019/882

Directive (EU) 2019/882–The European Accessibility Act (EAA), represents a significant expansion of accessibility obligations to all *non-public bodies*. Adopted in 2019, the directive aims to:

- Improve the quality of life for people with disabilities
- Promote social inclusion
- Ensure consistent accessibility standards across the European single market

The directive covers a wide range of digital and electronic products and services, including:

- E-commerce platforms
- Smartphones and computers
- ATMs and ticket machines
- Banking services
- E-books
- Online communication platforms

The directive's aim is to remove market fragmentation and reduce barriers that prevent users from accessing services and digital content across borders.

EN 301 549

EN 301 549 is the technical Implementation Standard to guide implementation. A technical standard explicitly defines how to meet both directives' requirements. It provides specifications for accessible design in software, websites, apps, and other ICT products. EN 301 549 fully adopts the WCAG criteria, particularly the success levels A and AA, as its baseline. EN 301 549's compliance ensures that any digital product also aligns with international accessibility norms.

National Law: The Implementation of EU Directives in Germany

Germany transposed EU directives 2016/2102 and 2019/882 into national law. The Act on Equal Opportunities for Persons with Disabilities (BGG) and Accessible Information Technology Ordinance (BITV) regulate the public sector's legal framework (EU 2016/2102), while the Accessibility Improvement Act (BFSG) regulates the private sector's (EU 2019/882).

BGG–the Act on Equal Opportunities for Persons with Disabilities

The BGG, enacted in 2002, aims to prevent the discrimination of people with disabilities and to ensure equal participation in social life. It primarily targets public institutions. Until the BFSG came into force, many private organisations used the BGG as a guideline for accessible design.

BITV–Accessible Information Technology Ordinance

The BITV specifies the technical requirements that public sector bodies must follow to ensure their digital services are accessible. It is based on § 12b BGG and aligns with WCAG standards, ensuring that German public services comply with internationally recognised accessibility criteria. The current version, BITV 2.0, applies to websites, mobile applications, and internal platforms of public institutions. It reflects WCAG requirements and ensures structured, perceivable, operable, understandable, and robust access to digital content for everyone.

BFSG–Accessibility Improvement Act

The BFSG, introduced in 2021 and entering full effect in 2025, enforces EU

Directive 2019/882 for the private sector in Germany. It applies to companies listed in Section 1 BFSG, with exceptions for micro-enterprises as defined in § 3 (3) BFSG.

Furthermore, companies are also required by § 14 (1), No. 2 with Annex 3 No. 1 BFSG to inform users—for example, in their general terms and conditions—about their services' fulfilment of accessibility obligations. This includes:

- A clear explanation of how the service fulfils the accessibility requirements of the BFSGV
- Clear information about the authority responsible for monitoring compliance

This transparency obligation is not only a regulatory requirement—it is a tool for accountability, allowing consumers, regulators, and advocacy Organisations to verify claims and encourage industry-wide adherence.

Conclusion

Digital accessibility is increasingly recognised as a global legal and ethical standard. From internationally accepted frameworks like the Web Content Accessibility Guidelines (WCAG) and ISO norms, to supranational regulations such as the European Accessibility Act, and national laws in countries around the world—there is a growing, unified commitment to ensuring equal access to digital systems for everyone.

A structured legal framework in Germany reflects this commitment: BGG, BITV for the public sector, and BFSG for the private sector, along with its technical specification, BFSGV[128]. These national laws translate EU directives into enforceable obligations, making accessibility a legal requirement for digital products and services across both public and commercial domains.

Globally, the message is clear: accessibility is not a technical add-on—it is a fundamental requirement for participation, equity, and inclusion in the digital age. Organisations that anticipate and implement these requirements proactively meet compliance expectations while also showing leadership in inclusive design, social responsibility, and long-term digital sustainability.

9.4 Inclusive Design Concepts: Beyond the Legal

While legal regulations define the minimum requirements for accessibility, inclusive design goes far beyond what is merely obligatory. It aims to make products, environments, and services usable for as many people as possible, regardless of their physical, cognitive, cultural, or social background.

This context features two core concepts: *Universal Design* and *Design for All.* Though closely aligned in purpose, they have different origins and nuances.

---

[128] "**Verordnung** über die Barrierefreiheitsanforderungen für Produkte und Dienstleistungen nach dem Barrierefreiheitsstärkungsgesetz" (Translation by the author: "***Ordinance** on Accessibility Requirements for Products and Services under the Accessibility Improving Act*").

Universal Design

Universal design originated in the United States and is based on the idea of creating products and environments that are inherently usable by everyone, without adaptation or specialised design. The concept focuses on general principles that ensure broad usability from the outset—designs that do not require additional effort to include marginalised users.[129]

This approach emphasises efficiency, equality, and user independence. Its strength lies in creating interfaces and experiences that work without exceptions, supporting a seamless interaction for everyone from the beginning.

Design for All

Design for All, developed more prominently in Europe, places greater emphasis on social justice and inclusion. It builds on the idea that design must reflect and support the diversity of human needs, including those of people with disabilities, older adults, children, and culturally diverse populations.[130]

While Universal Design focuses on functionality and broad application, Design for All brings ethical and societal dimensions into the spotlight—ensuring that everyone is included, not by chance, but by design. Participatory processes often involve including users early in the development cycle so they can voice their expectations and barriers.

Practical Example

Imagine an online hotel booking portal, built to WCAG 2.1 Level AA standards, provides alt texts for images, uses high contrast colours, supports screen readers, clearly describes links, labels all form fields, and avoids empty buttons. It meets legal accessibility requirements.

Building on this foundation, the portal also applies *Universal Design* or *Design for All* principles. It features, e.g. voice control, intuitive navigation with symbols, culturally sensitive icons, and personalised presets. The interface supports users of various ages, language backgrounds, and cognitive abilities—without requiring customisation or assistance. The goal is to create a truly inclusive experience that enables autonomy for the broadest possible range of users.

---

[129] Persson, Åhman, Yngling, & Gulliksen, 2014; Okabe & Ito, 2008; United Nations, 2006.
[130] Persson, Åhman, Yngling, & Gulliksen, 2014.

Conclusion

Inclusive Design is about more than technical compliance—it is about inclusivity, empowerment, and human dignity. It recognises the diversity of users as a strength and prioritises the needs of diverse users over designing for the average. By embracing holistic design principles like Universal Design and Design for All, designers, and companies expand their audience and contribute to a more accessible and future-ready digital society.

9.5 WCAG in Practice: The Relevant Criteria for UX

The Web Content Accessibility Guidelines provide a structured international standard for digital accessibility. They are technical specifications for developers and a valuable tool for UX and UI design. Four key principles guide accessible interaction and form the foundation of WCAG:

Four key principles of WCAG

Perceivable: Information and interface components must be presented in ways that users can perceive (e.g. through sight, hearing, or touch).
Operable: Interface and functionalities must be usable for everyone (via keyboard or assistive technologies as well).
Understandable: Content and controls must be clearly presented and predictable.
Robust: Applications and their content must be compatible with a wide range of user agents, including assistive technologies.

Due to the broad scope of WCAG, UX teams are not expected to address all 86 success criteria on their own. This section highlights those criteria that have the most direct and practical impact on user experience and inclusive design.

WCAG 1.1.1—Non-Text Content

WCAG 2.1 success criterion 1.1.1 requires that all non-text content—such as images, infographics, and diagrams—include text alternatives. These alternatives make the content accessible to users of screen readers or those with limited vision, and they also display when images fail to load due to technical issues.

Forms of image captioning include:[131]

- Alt attributes on <img> elements
- Visible text near the image
- Text on a separate page linked to the image
- A descriptive text link adjacent to the image

---

[131] WebAIM, 2021.

Decorative Images

Decorative images serve a purely visual purpose without conveying content.[132] In such cases, an empty alt attribute (alt="") ensures the screen reader skips them, avoiding unnecessary clutter for the user.

Logos

The alt text for a logo typically comprises the company's name. Including the word "logo" is unnecessary unless it provides a meaningful context for the user.

WCAG 1.4.3—Contrast (Minimum)

The legibility of text elements depends significantly on the contrast ratio between the foreground colour (usually text) and the adjacent colour (typically the background). Adequate contrast ensures that text is readable for people with visual impairments, including colour vision deficiencies, low vision, and age-related decline in contrast sensitivity. Adequate contrast also improves readability in low-light conditions or with reduced screen brightness.

Required Ratios

According to WCAG 2.1, the minimum contrast ratio between text and background is: **4.5:1** for normal-sized text and **3:1** for large-scale text (defined as 18 point regular or 14 point bold).

Exceptions

- Text content in an *inactive* (disabled) state (e.g. a greyed-out button) is exempt.
- Purely *decorative text* with no informational value (e.g. an artistic headline, stylised graphics, or watermarks) does not need to meet the contrast ratio requirement.

Optimal Range and User Comfort

While WCAG defines contrast ratios of **4.5:1** for normal text and **3:1** for large text as the minimum for accessibility, using the maximum contrast ratio of **21:1**—such as pure black on pure white (#000000 on #FFFFFF)—remains within technical guidelines. However, extremely high contrast can cause visual fatigue, especially during extended reading sessions or for neurodiverse users who are more sensitive to intense visual stimuli.

For optimal readability and comfort—particularly in body text or interfaces intended for prolonged use—a slightly softer contrast, such as dark grey on a light background (e.g. #333333 on #FFFFFF), is often more suitable. This still meets accessibility requirements while reducing strain.

[132] Yesilada & Harper, 2019.

Text Links and Interactive States

- **Colour-only distinction**: When colour is the only difference between a link and the surrounding text, ensure a minimum contrast ratio of **3:1** with the surrounding text and **4.5:1** against the background
- **Additional visual cues**: When links include other distinguishing features—such as underlines or **bold formatting**—the contrast with surrounding text may fall below **3:1**, as long as the background contrast still meets the **4.5:1** requirement.

Background on Contrast Standards

A contrast ratio of 3:1 is the minimum recommended contrast for text according to **ISO-9241-303** and **ANSI-HFES-100-1988**. This value is based on assumptions about people without visual impairments. However, WCAG 2.1 raises the requirement to 4.5:1 for standard text to account for real-world variations in visual perception. This increase stems from two key factors:

1. The **3:1 ratio** represents the minimum contrast that users with normal visual acuity **(20/20)** typically need in optimal conditions.

2. Experiences show those with **20/40**[133] vision, a typical mild impairment, have 1.5 times less contrast sensitivity than those with normal vision. Therefore, to ensure legibility for this group, the required contrast becomes:

$3 \times 1.5 =$ **4.5:1**

Similarly, people with **20/80 vision** need around **7:1** contrast to achieve the same legibility. These findings form the basis for the AA and AAA conformance levels in WCAG: 4.5:1 and 7:1, respectively.

Looking Ahead on Contrast Standards

The Accessible Perceptual Contrast Algorithm (APCA), under development by W3C's Accessibility Guidelines Working Group, is a more nuanced model based on perceptual readability rather than pure luminance ratios. It is being tested as a foundation for **WCAG 3.0**, to improve real-world readability across devices, light settings, and visual contexts.

Addressing Colour Deficiency

Globally, about *8 percent of men* and *0.5 percent of women* suffer from a colour deficiency, most commonly red-green deficiency.[134] Designers must avoid using colour alone to convey meaning. Instead, pair the colour with:

---

[133] **A visual acuity of 20/40**, in the European interpretation, means a level of sharpness that is about half as good as normal vision. A person with 20/40 vision can see details at a given distance that someone with normal vision (20/20) would see from twice as far away.

[134] Interessenverband der Farbsehschwachen und Farbenblinden e. V., 2024.

- Text labels
- Icons
- Patterns or shape indicators

This approach is especially vital for status indicators (e.g. success, error, warning) in dashboards, forms, and notifications.

Colour Vision Deficiency

Colour vision deficiency is a limited ability to distinguish certain colours. It is less severe than full colour blindness.

Colour Blindness

Colour Blindness is a more serious condition where affected individuals cannot differentiate between shades that are obvious to others. Experts estimate they perceive only about 10 percent of the hues and shades visible to those with normal colour vision.

The three main types of colour blindness are:

- **Deuteranopia:** Absence of green cone cells
- **Protanopia:** Absence of red cone cells
- **Tritanopia:** Absence of blue cone cells

One study noted that many affected individuals are unaware of their condition.[135] Another found that *1 in 5 Americans* only realise they are colourblind after high school or later in life.[136] This shows how infrequently doctors test for colour blindness.

Designing Accessible Colour Palettes

Inclusive interface design relies on three core principles:[137]

- **Sufficient contrast:** Choose colour palettes clearly perceived across all types of colour deficiencies, factoring in lighting and screen conditions. Rely more on differences in brightness than hue.
- **Combination of colour and additional visual cues:** Do not rely on colour alone. Use symbols, text, positions, line types, or patterns to support colour meaning.
- **Clear colour names:** Use familiar, standard colour names (e.g. cobalt blue, sun yellow) or established systems like RAL, Pantone, or W3C colour catalogs. Avoid ambiguous or artistic labels like "forest fairy green" that provide no functional reference.

[135] Basak & Roy, 2022.
[136] EnChroma, 2021.
[137] Vogel & Stahmann, 2024.

WCAG 1.4.11–Non-Text Contrast

While the criteria of WCAG 1.4.3 apply to contrasts in text content, WCAG 1.4.11 defines contrast specifically for *graphic elements* such as *icons, diagrams, radio buttons*, or checkboxes. These graphic elements may be static or interactive. Their contrast with adjacent colours must have a value of at least **3:1**.

Exceptions apply to:

- Control elements that are permanently or temporarily inactive (disabled)
- Graphic elements that are labeled and whose labeling itself maintains the required contrast to the adjacent colour
- Logos, flags, snapshots, or photos where the designer has no influence on the design

States

Defining interactive states is an essential part of UX design. Visual feedback provides users with reliable orientation and control. WCAG 1.4.11 mandates that interactive graphic elements and their various states must be equally perceptible to all users. States such as Default, Hover, Pressed, Focused, Active, etc., must each maintain a minimum contrast ratio of 3:1 to their background. For example, a default state with colour #191919 on a white background (#FFFFFF) yields a contrast ratio of 17.58:1, which fully meets WCAG requirements.

Changes of State

The contrast difference between interactive states themselves (e.g. from default to hover) **does not need to meet** the same contrast requirement. Instead, it is only necessary that each individual state meet the 3:1 contrast rule in relation to the background. In the example above, a hover state of #303030 on white results in a contrast ratio of 13.2:1. Though the difference between states is only 1.33:1, both values independently meet the standard.

However, despite technical compliance, such subtle differences may still cause usability issues. Insufficient contrast between interactive states makes state transitions unclear, leading to orientation problems, confusion, and frustration. This significantly harms the user experience for users with any kind of disability. Thus, it is strongly recommended to ensure that contrast between states is also visually distinct, even if not formally required. This improves accessibility and orientation for all users.

Interactive Buttons

According to WCAG 1.4.11, interactive buttons do not necessarily need a visible border or fill colour unless such features show interactivity. For example, in a text button, the contrast of the text or symbol alone is sufficient—provided it meets the contrast threshold. If the button includes both text and a border or fill, then either the text/symbol or the graphic features must meet the 3:1 contrast requirement.

Diagrams

A common example is a pie chart. It visually communicates proportions as segments of a circle, each representing a part of a whole. These segments must also meet contrast requirements:

- Each segment should contrast at least 3:1 against neighboring areas, *or*
- adequate contrast in corresponding labels is necessary, *or*
- equivalent information must be available elsewhere (e.g. a legend below the chart).

WCAG and 2.5.8–Target Size

The WCAG Guidelines 2.5.5 (Target Size) and 2.5.8 (Target Size-Minimum) define requirements for the minimum size of interactive elements. These guidelines ensure the accessibility and usability of control elements, such as buttons, links, and other interactive areas. Sufficiently sized target areas make operation easier and reduce the error rate due to unintentional input errors. In particular, people with motor impairments or those who use touchscreens benefit from larger and easily accessible interactive areas.

WCAG 2.5.5 requires that interactive elements have a minimum size of 44 × 44 pixels. This corresponds to the AAA conformance level and aims to ensure optimal accessibility. WCAG 2.5.8 is based on the AA conformance level and allows a reduced target size of 24 × 24 pixels. This defines a minimum requirement that may not offer optimal ease of use but still ensures appropriate accessibility.

Minimum and Optimum

WCAG 2.5.8 represents the "minimum" requirement, while WCAG 2.5.5 reflects the "optimum" level of accessibility for pointer gestures. The reason for this is that elements smaller than 44 × 44 pixels may be too small for operation.

Studies, such as those by the Nielsen Norman Group,[138] show that touchscreens benefit from larger target sizes, as these enable more precise and faster inputs and reduce errors. The Nielsen Norman Group therefore recommends a target area of at least 1 × 1 cm, which corresponds to almost 44 pixels. Google[139], Microsoft[140], and Apple[141] among other large companies, recommend minimum interactive element sizes of 40 × 40 to 48 × 48 pixels.

Besides the target size, the distance between interactive elements is also relevant. Areas that are too close together increase the risk of unintentional clicks and impair usability. A clickable area of 24 × 24 pixels or 44 × 44 pixels meets the requirements of WCAG 2.5.5 and 2.5.8.

---

[138] Harley, 2019.
[139] Google, 2025.
[140] Microsoft, 2021.
[141] Apple, 2024.

Exception–Continuous Text

Interactive elements placed within body text are exceptions to the target size rules. These include text links or info icons. Such elements do not need to meet the specified size requirements, as the primary focus here lies on optimal readability.

The WCAG 2.5.5 and 2.5.8 guidelines complement each other by defining minimum standards and optimal recommendations for the usability of interactive elements. They promote an accessible and user-friendly design that minimises input errors and enables precise interaction for everyone. The balance between minimum requirements and optimal design supports broad accessibility without restricting readability or functionality.

WCAG 2.2.2 – Pause, Exit, Hide

This guideline aims to reduce barriers caused by automatically moving, flashing or updating content. This ensures such content is not perceived as disruptive or confusing, guaranteeing accessible use.

According to WCAG 2.2.2, content that moves, flashes, scrolls or refreshes automatically for *over five seconds* must provide users with a mechanism to pause, stop, or hide the movement. Specifically, the content must be able to be paused, stopped, or hidden by the user. Such elements include:

- Sliders (carousels)
- Animated advertisements
- Automatically played videos

This regulation does not apply if the movement or update is an essential part of the activity. This includes live-updated content, such as livestock market prices or sports results.

Implementation in User Experience Design

- Provide clearly visible controls to pause, stop, or hide the movement
- Offer accessible controls, with appropriate size and sufficient contrast

This is important in designs with autoplay features—such as carousels or background animations—which may unintentionally distract or disorient users. Following accessibility principles ensures that everyone can reliably use the controls.

WCAG 2.4.7 and 2.4.13–Focus Visible

This success criterion ensures people navigating via keyboard can always recognise which interactive element is currently active. This is especially important for users with motor impairments or visual disabilities. Everyone can benefit in situations where a navigation mouse is temporarily unavailable or nonfunctional.

Focus Indicator

A focus indicator is a visual cue that highlights the currently focused element. This typically appears as a border around the focused component.

Implementation in User Experience Design

The "focus visible" state plays a crucial role in UX design and deserves attention when defining the states of interface components. Two common implementations exist:

- **Automatically generated standard browser indicators**: The browser activates these if the CSS rule outline: none is not applied. While they require no additional setup, the indicators often vary between browsers and rarely match a brand's visual guidelines.
- **Custom-designed focus indicators**: These allow the design team to align the focus styles with the brand identity and overall design language, ensuring a consistent and accessible user experience.

Targeted Use of Focus Indicators

Focus indicators should appear only during keyboard navigation. It often appears mistakenly during mouse selection or when a field becomes active, creating a conflict between focus and active states. Switching **":focus"** to **":focus-visible"** in the CSS will fix this.

Visual Representation and Contrast

The definition of visual representation is not based on WCAG 1.4.7, but on WCAG 1.4.13, which corresponds to the highest conformance level AAA. This means that contrast and visual presentation are only mandatory for digital applications that explicitly commit to implementing the highest WCAG accessibility level.

However, poor contrast can significantly impair perceptibility, which is why many teams adopt these criteria as a standard, regardless of whether they are mandatory.

According to WCAG 1.4.13, the focus indicator must be at least as large as a 2-pixel outline around the unfocused component. The most common representation is as a border, either within the component or further outside. Adjacent colour is determined by the indicator's position. The recommendation is a contrast value of at least 3:1 to the surrounding colours.

One exception applies when the presentation program defines the component's appearance, and the design does not override it. In this case, standard browser indicators are exempt from the requirement, even if they do not meet the contrast ratio. So, if standard focus indicators lack sufficient contrast with surrounding colours, they still comply with this criterion.

Conclusion and Recommendations

A clearly visible and functional focus indicator is fundamental for accessibility and contributes significantly to a better user experience. Although browser defaults offer quick implementation, they often fall short in meeting both design aesthetics and accessibility needs.

Therefore, **customised focus indicators** are preferable, because they ensure:

- Brand consistency
- Compliance with contrast and visibility guidelines
- Reliable usability across browsers

Additional recommendations include:

- Use ":focus-visible" to limit visibility of focus indicators to keyboard navigation.
- Design custom indicators in alignment with corporate style guides.
- Ensure a minimum contrast of 3:1 and a visible area of at least 2 pixels around the component.

Other Important WCAG Guidelines for User Experience

Below you will find a few more regulations that deserve a closer look in user experience design:

- **WCAG 1.2.2** Subtitles (A) and **WCAG 1.2.1** Audio transcript (A): To ensure everyone understands the content, provide video and audio files with subtitles or transcripts. This offers a text alternative, benefiting those with hearing difficulties or in situations where sound or video is not accessible.
- **WCAG 1.4.4 Customizable text (AA):** Ensure that texts scale up to 200 percent without losing functionality or content, allowing people with visual impairments to access content more easily without compromising usability.
- **WCAG 1.4.5 Text in images (AA):** Avoid placing text within images, as it often reduces readability and creates difficulties when enlarged or viewed on various devices. When including text in images is necessary, ensure sufficient contrast between the text and background to maintain optimal readability.
- **WCAG 2.1.1 Keyboard accessibility (A):** Ensure all functions of a digital application are fully accessible using a keyboard. This allows users to navigate and interact with the interface without a mouse—crucial for people with motor impairments or those using screen readers.
- **WCAG 2.4.4 Link purpose (A)**: Make the purpose of each link clear through its text or surrounding context. This helps users understand where a link leads or what action it will trigger.
- **WCAG 2.4.6 Headings and captions (AA):** Use headings and labels that clearly describe the topic or function of each section or element. This supports faster navigation and better orientation.
- **WCAG 3.2.3 Consistent navigation (AA)**: Ensure predictability and

consistency for users. Websites and applications must always present recurring navigation mechanisms in the same order.

- **WCAG 3.2.4 Consistent identification (AA):** Present elements consistently across multiple pages if they serve the same function. Consistent design enhances learnability and usability.
- **WCAG 3.3.1 Error identification (A)** and **WCAG 3.3.3 Error description (AA):** When users submit a form with missing or incorrect information, ensure the interface automatically highlights the affected fields and provides clear text descriptions of the issues. Where possible, include suggestions to help users correct the input and proceed without barriers.

Conclusion

The WCAG guidelines play a central role in the design of accessible digital applications. They are based on the four principles of perceptibility, operability, understandability, and robustness and contain many criteria that are specifically aimed at ensuring an inclusive user experience.

Particularly relevant aspects include providing of text alternatives for non-text content, sufficient contrast ratios, clear focus indicators, and adequate target sizes for interactive elements. These measures enable people with different needs to use digital content on an equal footing.

For an optimal user experience, go beyond meeting minimum requirements and aim for solutions that are both aesthetically and functionally strong. Consistently applying WCAG guidelines enhances accessibility and also improves overall user-friendliness.

9.6 Easy and Plain Language

Easy language is a simplified way of writing that makes content easier to read and understand for people with cognitive impairments or learning challenges. This is beneficial for individuals with limited reading skills, low language proficiency, or intellectual disabilities. Easy language helps ensure that written content is accessible for all, promoting inclusion and a sense of belonging.

Besides easy language, there is plain language, which targets a broader audience—including people with reading difficulties or limited command of the specific language. Unlike easy language, plain language is not governed by fixed rules, but guided by recommendations.

Norms and Standards for Easy Language

Internationally, IFLA: *Guidelines for Easy-to-Read Materials* provide principles for writing accessible content.[142] These internationally recognised guidelines offer principles for creating accessible written content across different cultures and contexts, particularly in libraries and public communication.

In Germany, various sets of rules define easy language. Organisations like

[142] Nomura, Nielsen & Tronbacke, 2010.

Netzwerk Leichte Sprache e.V.[143], Inclusion Europe[144], and BITV 2.0 provide a solid basis for implementing easy language in practice. The German Institute for Standardisation offers a higher-level recommendation: **DIN SPEC 33429**[145], which includes guidelines for translations, writing, and content design in easy language.

Norms and Standards for Plain Language

For a global audience, one of the most widely recognised references for plain language is the *Plain Language Association International* (PLAIN). PLAIN defines plain language as communication in which wording, structure, and design are so clear that the intended audience easily finds what they need, understands it, and uses it.[146] PLAIN is a founding member of the International Plain Language Federation (IPLF) and plays a central role in shaping international standards.

In 2023, the International Organization for Standardization (ISO) published **ISO 24495-1 – Plain Language – Part 1**,[147] the first global standard for plain language. It outlines governing principles and guidelines for written communication across all sectors and languages.[148] The ISO standard builds on PLAIN's foundational work and provides a structured, internationally recognised framework for creating accessible, user-friendly content. Together, PLAIN and ISO 24495-1 offer comprehensive guidance for developing clear and inclusive communication, helping Organisations reach a wide range of audiences effectively and accessibly.

In Germany, there is a specific national standard: **DIN 8581-1**, which complements the ISO standard by providing additional guidance tailored to the German language and legal context.[149] The following section draws on these standards while also incorporating global best practices in easy and plain language design.

Recommendations for easy language

- **Use familiar, everyday vocabulary**: Choose words that are commonly understood. Avoid jargon, legalese, and unexplained technical terms. If complex terms are necessary, explain them clearly (e.g. "migraine means a very severe headache").
- **Avoid synonyms and figurative language**: Avoid using metaphors or idioms unless they are widely understood or you explain them with concrete language.
- **Use short, direct sentences**: Aim for simple sentence structures: one main idea per sentence, using a clear subject-verb-object order.
- **Avoid complex syntax**: Steer clear of long, nested sentences, and

[143] https://www.netzwerk-leichte-sprache.de/
[144] Inclusion Europe, 2017.
[145] Deutsches Institut für Normung, 2023.
[146] Plain Language Association International, 2025.
[147] ISO - International Organization for Standardization, 2023.
[148] See design guidelines at: International Plain Language Federation, 2025.
[149] Deutsches Institut für Normung, 2024.

minimise relative clauses or passive constructions.
- **Organise content logically**: Group related information into clear sections. Use meaningful subheadings, bullet points, and white space to aid navigation.
- **Support reading flow:** Structure text into short paragraphs. Provide a table of contents for longer documents.
- **Design visually for clarity**: Use legible fonts and appropriate font sizes. Choose high-contrast text and background combinations for readability.
- **Add explanatory images or icons**: Use visuals to reinforce written content, especially for complex topics.
- **Avoid negations:** Rephrase sentences to state what users should do instead of what they shouldn't (e.g. "Remember to take your medicine" instead of "Do not forget...").
- **Use simple verb tenses**: Avoid using future and conditional tenses when they might reduce clarity.

Visual Design According to DIN SPEC 33429 and Global Standards

Visual structure and layout are just as important as wording. Recommend to DIN SPEC 33429:2023-04 and plain language advocates worldwide:

- Organise content clearly with consistent visual hierarchy
- Use accessible fonts and sufficient contrast between text and background
- Apply layout techniques that support scanability and comprehension
- Provide alternative text for visual content

Conclusion

Easy and plain language are key elements of inclusive design. This allows people with diverse backgrounds and varying abilities to access information and participate equally, bridging language barriers.

While global standards such as the IFLA Guidelines for easy language and ISO 24495-1 for plain language provide broad, internationally recognised guidance, Germany complements these frameworks with its own national standards—notably DIN SPEC 33429 for easy language and DIN 8581-1 for plain language. These German standards offer additional specificity tailored to linguistic and legal contexts within the country. By applying these standards, using well-structured language, and integrating supportive visual elements, communication becomes more accessible, understandable, and inclusive for everyone.

9.7 Gender-Inclusive Communication

> *"The limits of my language mean the limits of my world."*
>
> (Ludwig Wittgenstein, translated by the author)

In a diverse society, it is essential to use inclusive language that welcomes everyone—and ensures no one feels excluded. Gender-inclusive language is both a linguistic concern and a matter of social justice, reflecting the awareness of diverse identities.

Language and society influence one another; changes in one often drive changes in the other. Across many cultures, language has historically reflected power structures that favoured certain groups while marginalising others. Language defines how we describe and address people—and, by extension, how we acknowledge them. But identity changes, and language changes alongside it.

Many languages grammatically embed gender—especially in job titles, pronouns, and personal references. English, while structurally more neutral, still carries gendered assumptions in terms like "*fireman*" or "*chairman*", which require conscious attention.

Global Linguistic Challenges

Linguistic challenges vary considerably depending on the region and language family. In English-speaking contexts, gender inclusivity often faces fewer structural barriers, as many occupational and descriptive terms are already gender neutral. However, many Slavic languages (e.g. Polish, Russian, Czech) and Roman languages (e.g. Italian, French, or Spanish) embed grammatical gender deeply into their sentence structures. In these systems, inclusive language requires deliberate reformulation—and often sparks broader societal and political debates.

Yet even in places without formal requirements for inclusive language, the ethical value of addressing everyone—not only a presumed binary or default "male" audience—makes inclusive communication essential. Language must reflect the people it speaks to.

Key Principles of Gender-Inclusive Communication

This section is based on recommendations from the *European Institute for Gender Equality*[150] and *Council of Europe's Guidelines for the use of language as a driver of inclusivity.*[151]

- **Avoid gender-biased or discriminatory language**: Language often reflects outdated or stereotypical gender roles. Use terms that do not reinforce these roles or exclude certain identities. Replace expressions like "*mankind*" with "*humankind,*" "*manpower*" with "*workforce,*" and "*Dear Sir or Madam*" with "*To whom it may concern*" or "*Dear colleagues*".
- **Use gender neutral job titles and descriptions:** Avoid implying gender-specific roles. Use "*chair*" instead of "*chairman*", "*flight attendant*" instead of "*stewardess*", and "*business executive*" instead of "*businessman*". In gendered languages, consider paired forms "*Studenten und Studentinnen*" or inclusive neologisms "*Studierende*"

[150] European Institute for Gender Equality, 2024.
[151] Council of Europe., 2024.

- **Use inclusive pronouns:** Adopt gender-neutral pronouns like singular "*they*" when gender is unknown or irrelevant. For example, write "*Each student must submit their paper*". Respect individuals chosen pronouns and, where possible, avoid defaulting to "*he*" or "*she*"
- **Make gender visible when it counters stereotypes:** Highlight gender deliberately to challenge historical exclusion or underrepresentation, such as "*Female scientists have contributed significantly*" or "*Applications from men, women, and non-binary candidates are welcome*"
- **Avoid reinforcing stereotypical gender roles in context:** Ensure that language and imagery portray a range of people in varied roles. Avoid depicting only women in caregiving positions or only men in leadership. Represent all genders in both professional and domestic contexts.
- **Adapt inclusive language to local contexts:** Inclusive communication must be sensitive to grammatical and social norms. For example, use "*Lehrende*" in German—a gender-neutral term for educators that avoids masculine or feminine forms—or explore emerging inclusive forms in Slavic languages—always aligning with cultural understanding and clarity.

Conclusion

Inclusive language is not only an ethical concern—it is a practical one. It shapes accessibility, trust, and emotional tone across all forms of communication. Whether in user interfaces, instruction manuals, event invitations, or internal policies, how we address others directly affects who feels acknowledged and respected. Gender-inclusive communication contributes to a broader sense of belonging. It affirms identity, avoids exclusion, and supports fairness. By aligning our language with the diversity of real people, we enable communication that is more accurate and more humane.

This is not about linguistic perfection. It is about awareness, empathy, and the willingness to adapt how we speak to help build a more open, inclusive world—online and offline.

9.8 Summary and Critical Reflection

Digital accessibility and inclusion are more than technical requirements—they represent a fundamental commitment to equality. Designing digital applications accessibly is a legal necessity in many countries and a global key element of sustainable user experience.

The principles of perceivability, operability, understandability, and robustness—which are the core principles of WCAG—provide the foundation for making digital products usable for everyone, regardless of physical, cognitive, or sensory abilities. Legal frameworks such as Germany's BFSG and international standards like WCAG and ISO have made accessibility a binding obligation across public and private sectors. The upcoming WCAG 3.0 will raise expectations further, shifting toward a more user-centered and outcome-based model that reflects evolving technologies and real-world contexts.

This progress, however, presents major challenges for small and medium-sized enterprises (SME). While large organisations often have dedicated resources and technical teams, SME frequently lack the capacity, funding, or clarity to implement accessibility measures effectively. The increasing complexity of standards like WCAG 3.0 risks widening the gap between regulatory ambition and what SME can realistically deliver. For accessibility to succeed, it must be supported by clear guidance, affordable tools, and targeted implementation support.

Yet accessibility is not just about meeting technical standards. It is a dynamic, evolving process rooted in ethical values, social responsibility, and human-centered design. Inclusive, easy and plain language, and gender-sensitive communication must be considered alongside interactive design, visual presentation, and technological compatibility.

Accessibility is not a static state, but an ongoing commitment. As technologies advance and user expectations shift, companies, and development teams must remain open to learning, re-evaluating assumptions, and engaging in dialogue with affected communities.

Accessibility is not a constraint, but an opportunity: to build better, more humane, and more sustainable digital products.

10 MANAGEMENT APPROACHES FOR SUSTAINABLE UX

Every year, the Deloitte CxO Sustainability Reports[152] examine the goals and actions of around 2,000 executives worldwide in relation to sustainability. A key finding from recent years is the divergence between ambition and implementation. Although organisations increasingly recognise sustainability as a strategic success factor, many still face significant obstacles:

- Limited integration of sustainability into business strategies
- Unclear responsibilities within organisations
- Lack of consistent standards
- Regulatory uncertainties
- Limited resources

In 2022, climate change was perceived as an urgent threat, and many organisations already felt its impact. Still, transformative action remained limited. Short-term costs were cited as a major barrier. In 2023, awareness of the need for systemic change increased significantly – driven by stakeholders and employees. Investment in sustainability rose, and long-term strategic value became more widely recognised. The 2024 report shows a clear shift: sustainability is now widely regarded as a driver of innovation and value creation, with a growing emphasis on its financial benefits.

10.1 Integrating Sustainability Into the Company

Despite existing challenges, there is a clear trend: sustainability is increasingly becoming an integral part of business strategies. In recent years, it has established itself as a key quality feature and plays a strategically important role for companies. Ideally, holistic integration begins with the corporate vision and mission statements. To ensure ecological, social, and economic considerations are equally important in all innovations and process optimisations, we need to consistently integrate this orientation into our strategy and innovation culture.

Svenja Stöveken, Head of the Strategy business unit and an expert on strategy and sustainability, has analysed over 100 companies that have already integrated sustainability into their strategies.[153] She has identified nine key

[152] Deloitte Global, 2021, 2022, 2023, 2024.
[153] Stöveken & Brugger, 2018.

areas of opportunity that help companies link sustainability and profitability. These opportunities fall into two main categories.

The first category includes strategic approaches aimed at a fair economy:

- Improving access to sustainable products
- Redesigning business models by providing products as services
- Integrating the consumer society and stakeholders more closely into sustainable value chains

Companies can also extend their reach by gaining a new target audience for sustainable products or by restructuring parts of their product and service portfolio to be more sustainable.

The second category focuses on circular economy strategies, which promote the efficient use of resources and the reduction of waste:

- Extending product lifespans through repair and reuse strategies
- Recovering and reusing materials (recycling)
- Replacing conventional raw materials with more sustainable alternatives (substitution)
- Reducing energy and material consumption through greater eco-efficiency

Companies can also minimise resource use by converting emissions and waste materials into new, innovative products (a process called conversion).

These nine areas of opportunity clarify that companies have far more ways to integrate sustainability into their business strategies than just focusing on ecological aspects. Rather, the aim is to develop a holistic sustainability strategy that protects the environment and brings economic benefits.

Stöveken emphasizes that companies seeking to embed sustainability strategically must implement targeted measures and position sustainability as a core element of their corporate strategy. This also includes the active involvement of all employees and the creation of a corporate culture that consistently promotes sustainable principles. Long-term competitive advantages only arise from company-wide sustainability integration.

Three steps are essential to ensure the long-term integration of sustainability:

- Align corporate strategies with sustainability goals
- Embed sustainability into internal company processes
- Implement systematic methods for measuring and evaluating progress

Top-Down and Bottom-Up: Building Sustainable Strategy

Integrating sustainability depends on the size and structure of the company. Smaller companies have the advantage of flatter hierarchies but often have fewer resources. In medium-sized companies, resources are generally sufficient; however, limited flexibility in internal processes can hinder implementation. In large companies, there are usually more complex structures and fixed, formal processes, which often makes change processes slower and more complex. Shifting direction may originate from leadership (top-down) or from the teams (bottom-up) themselves.

Bottom-Up Approach

Operational teams often spot clear areas for improvement and offer ideas for lasting changes and alternative approaches. This strategy works best with intrinsically motivated teams and a corporate culture that embraces change. Bottom-up initiatives have the advantage that they are practical and creative and often embedded directly in the work processes. However, there is a risk that the measures will remain isolated and without strategic anchoring if management does not actively support and scale them.

But how can we convince managers of the benefits of a sustainable user experience?

Convincing managers of the value of sustainable user experiences requires careful preparation—starting with a deep understanding of their perspective and priorities. When arguments speak directly to business goals, efficiency, and strategic relevance, they are more likely to resonate. The following points help connect sustainability with leadership concerns:

- **Strategic advantages**: Show how sustainable UX improves competitive standing via higher user satisfaction and stronger brand image.
- **Cost-benefit analysis**: Provide at least a rough estimate of the financial advantages: e.g. lower bounce rates (through reduced cognitive load, simplified content, faster load times), improved acceptance based on ethical alignment, or more efficient processes via reusable design elements.
- **Clear ROI perspective**: Present how investments in sustainable UX generate returns—through increased user loyalty, lower support costs, and reduced abandonment rates. Use concrete scenarios and benchmarks to illustrate the potential benefits and the risks of inaction.
- **Long-term benefits**: Highlight how sustainable UX supports long-term goals such as customer loyalty, innovation capability, and brand value.
- **Measurable outcomes**: Data and success stories are convincing proof points. Managers appreciate visible, evidence-based results.
- **Implementation proposal**: A clear, step-by-step action plan makes the topic approachable and reduces resistance. Achieving small early wins can increase support.

Top-Down Initiative

When leadership actively drives the integration of sustainability, the approach gains strategic clarity and dedicated resources. Executives who prioritise sustainability, allocate budgets, and shape corporate culture create the conditions for systematic implementation. This positions sustainability as a core element of corporate strategy and everyday operations.

Roadmap Example

Awareness (Q1): Conduct workshops and training sessions for the UX team and other relevant departments, focusing on the core principles and strategic goals of sustainable UX. Use these sessions to build cross-functional awareness and foster shared responsibility.
Pilot project definition (Q2): Define specific sustainability criteria and success targets. Review existing digital products to identify areas with optimisation potential based on ecological, social, or ethical aspects.
Integration (Q3): Embed sustainability criteria into internal design systems and apply them in an initial pilot project. Use this phase to actively optimise selected components or workflows.
Evaluation (Q4): Assess the effectiveness of implemented measures using predefined sustainability metrics. Share results transparently and use them to support broader implementation of sustainability efforts across the organisation.

Recipe for Success–The Right Balance Between Bottom-Up and Top-Down
The most effective approach combines strategic direction from leadership with practical, innovative input from operational teams. When both levels contribute actively, the organisation fosters a culture where sustainability is deeply rooted and continuously reinforced.

Anchoring Sustainability in the Company's Own Processes

To ensure sustainability not merely a strategic vision, the company must consistently embed sustainability in its internal structures and daily operations. This means translating overarching sustainability goals into concrete, department-specific processes—especially in areas that directly influence digital products, such as UX design, development, and product management.

One of the key challenges lies in the tendency of many departments to focus narrowly on short-term project goals and KPIs. Sustainability frequently competes with time constraints, cost pressures, and legacy processes. The following steps foster successful integration of sustainability into departmental processes, including areas such as user experience:

- **Creating clarity about sustainability goals and values**: To anchor sustainability in processes, teams first define clear and measurable sustainability goals. These goals form the basis for all future decisions. Managers and their teams align on a shared understanding of sustainability and identify the specific outcomes they achieve. Joint meetings using the design thinking method help shape these definitions and objectives.
- **Integration of sustainability into the departments' strategy:** Sustainability should be an integral part of the strategic orientation across

all departments, rather than being treated as an additional task. Each department—whether user experience, marketing, or development—actively analyses and adapts its processes in line with defined sustainability goals. Targeted training and integration into goal-setting processes embed sustainability as a natural foundation for all decisions.
- **Stakeholder communication:** Considering stakeholder interests plays a key role in achieving long-term integration. Transparent communication around sustainability ensures that all stakeholders understand the environmental and social impacts of their decisions. This awareness strengthens commitment to sustainable practices and encourages active engagement. Stakeholder acceptance of sustainability grows substantially when ethical and economic value become visible.

The goal is to move from isolated sustainable gestures to *systemic integration*. This means that sustainability becomes a standard across teams—in terms of ecological concerns, and as a guiding principle for ethical, user-centered, and future-ready digital product development.

Implement Systematic Methods for Measuring and Evaluating Progress

To monitor the success and impact of sustainability initiatives, we need to develop measurable indicators and assessment methods. Metrics ensure that integrating sustainability remains effective in the long term.

- **Transparency and traceability**: Metrics enable companies to present their sustainability progress transparently. These metrics specifically measure the achievement of sustainable goals. Without clear metrics, it is difficult to assess the success or failure of sustainability strategies.
- **Continuous improvement**: Systematic measurement allows companies to identify weaknesses and potentials for improvement early. Regular monitoring of sustainability efforts allows companies to adjust their strategies and better meet their goals.
- **Responsibility and accountability**: establishing clear metrics creates a foundation for accountability with internal and external stakeholders. These metrics allow companies to show sustainability performance and build trust in their long-term strategic direction.
- **Long-term anchoring of sustainability**: integrating metrics into business processes ensures that sustainability remains a visible and actively managed part of daily operations. Systematic measurement helps prevent the strategy from fading into the background and ensures that sustainability continues to receive the attention needed to drive long-term impact.
- **Targeted control and decision support**: Clear key performance indicators guide the targeted management of resources and priorities. Metrics support informed decision-making, helping managers determine which sustainability measures to expand and which to phase out.

Establishing metrics ensures that sustainability moves beyond abstract goals and takes shape through concrete, verifiable actions and results. This approach anchors sustainability as a long-term, deeply embedded element of corporate strategy rather than a short-term initiative.

10.2 Management and Teams: Sharing Responsibility

Management and teams play crucial but different roles in integrating sustainability. While management makes strategic decisions and sets the course for sustainable initiatives, the teams are responsible for the practical implementation. However, their cooperation is essential for the success of sustainable integration.

The Role of Management

Management bears the primary responsibility for anchoring sustainability in user experience at a strategic level and for creating the conditions for successful implementation. Key responsibilities involve setting long-term, measurable goals, securing budgets, and ensuring the availability of necessary resources within the teams.

Another key management task involves creating structural frameworks that integrate sustainability principles into daily workflows and decision-making processes. This also means embedding sustainable criteria into project briefings, requirements, and approval steps. Sharing success stories and highlighting positive examples of sustainable practices strengthens motivation across teams.

The Role of Teams

Teams take responsibility for applying sustainability principles in their daily work and embedding them into operational processes. Engaging the entire team from the start helps spot and solve problems early, leading to a more efficient and effective outcome. When teams actively embrace sustainability, they generate more grounded and creative solutions that align directly with their workflows.

Shared Success: Cooperation Between Management and Teams

Successful sustainability integration relies on close collaboration between management and teams. Management assigns responsibility for execution while providing the autonomy needed to develop and test creative solutions. Ongoing training and a culture that values innovation strengthens this collaboration and reinforces sustainable practices across the organisation.

Colaborative goal setting and clear key performance indicators (KPIs) help both management and teams maintain a shared direction. Regular review sessions—based on qualitative feedback and quantitative metrics—keep the strategy dynamic and adaptable to changing or evolving needs and insights.

This joint effort lays the groundwork for a truly integrated, sustainable user experience that combines strategic vision with practical application.

10.3 Interdisciplinary Collaboration

Interdisciplinary collaboration in companies plays a critical role in innovation and problem-solving. It brings together expertise and perspectives from various disciplines, bridging traditional silos that often separate departments and hinder communication and empathy. The opposite of interdisciplinarity is silo thinking—where each team operates in isolation, concerned only with its own tasks and goals without a shared understanding of the larger context.

From Silo Thinking to Collaboration

The "silo" metaphor describes a structure in which departments or teams operate as self-contained units. In practice, this might look like:

- Product management collects requirements which they then pass to the team—often without full context or clarity.
- Project management coordinates communication and requirements, but misunderstandings still occur due to inconsistent clarity.
- UX teams design without input from development, overlooking technical implications.
- Development focuses solely on implementation, disconnected from user needs or sustainability concerns.
- Testing reveasl inconsistencies only at the end, causing delays and frustration.

A disjointed process often leads to inefficient workflows, missed opportunities for innovation, and increased environmental impact resulting from unnecessary iterations or poor decision-making.

True interdisciplinary collaboration addresses these challenges. A shared goal, mutual empathy for the user, and trust among teams enable faster and more effective implementation of solutions. This collaborative approach forms a crucial foundation for sustainable UX.

Interdisciplinarity

Interdisciplinarity refers to the purposeful collaboration of individuals from different disciplines to address shared questions. It involves integrating knowledge, methods, and perspectives from various fields to analyse and solve complex problems. The goal is to create a new, shared understanding that connects insights of the participating disciplines. Interdisciplinarity is a key driver of innovation and a critical success factor.

Nevertheless, there are only a few empirical studies that examine which principles and factors contribute to the success of interdisciplinary collaboration. One reason may be that such collaborations strongly depend on varying contextual conditions and specific team dynamics. Dissertations such as those by Brandstädter, along with project-based field reports, help bridge existing knowledge gaps in this area.[154]

Key principles for successful interdisciplinary work include:

- Defining shared goals and visions
- Understanding the different disciplines involved
- Establishing transparent communication structures
- Being open to flexibility and compromise

Challenges in Interdisciplinary Collaborations

Despite the promising benefits of interdisciplinary collaboration, teams face a range of challenges that require deliberate attention to achieve productive outcomes and enable effective cooperation:

- **Hierarchies and power structures:** An unequal or unclear distribution of responsibility and influence within an interdisciplinary team can create tensions—especially when individual disciplines overemphasise their own perspective or overlook the contributions of others. This disrupts team dynamics and puts the overall success of the project at risk.
- **Communication barriers:** Conveying complex, discipline-specific content requires both deep expertise and the ability to communicate in ways that are understandable to those from other fields. Without active exchange, team members may work in isolation, leaving valuable synergies untapped.
- **Time and resources:** Interdisciplinary collaboration demands time for alignment and reflection. Without sufficient organisational and financial support, projects risk stalling or falling short of their goals due to time constraints.

Solution Approaches to Challenges

To overcome these hurdles:

- Promote team skills in communication and conflict resolution training
- Clearly define roles and responsibilities
- Use collaborative tools to enhance transparency
- Foster an inclusive culture that values all disciplines equally
- Secure adequate time and funding for collaborative efforts

Assembling Interdisciplinary Teams

The composition of interdisciplinary teams depends on factors such as task complexity, project scope, and company size. For complex, multi-layered initiatives, teams benefit from working together from the outset toward a shared goal. When tasks become especially demanding, organisations often create several interdisciplinary teams, each responsible for a specific subtask. These groups regularly exchange insights and updates in joint meetings to

---

[154] Brandstädter, 2019.

maintain coherence and alignment across the broader initiative.

In less complex projects or smaller organisations, forming permanent teams with representatives from every relevant field is not always practical. Still, involving diverse expertise, even on a smaller scale, enriches perspectives and improves outcomes. In these cases, companies benefit from establishing regular interdisciplinary meetings or structured exchange formats. This approach allows leaner teams to harness the strengths of interdisciplinary collaboration, ensuring that diverse viewpoints actively shape both innovation and problem-solving.

Conclusion

Interdisciplinary work unlocks innovation and improves problem-solving by integrating diverse expertise. Clear goals, defined roles, and a supportive culture transform interdisciplinary collaboration into a powerful tool for sustainable UX, surpassing what isolated teams can accomplish.

10.4 Sustainable Corporate Culture

However, such a culture demands more than technological adjustments. It requires a mindset shift across the entire organisation—from management to individual departments. It starts with awareness building and team involvement, and extends to clear guidelines and continuous improvement processes. This demands targeted strategies to foster change at every level of the organisation.

B. J. Fogg's Behavior Model provides a robust framework here, defining motivation, ability, and triggers as core components for sustainable behaviour change.[155] These principles support the implementation of sustainable practices and help ensure their long-term adoption.

Motivation

Motivation is essential for teams and management to commit to sustainable processes. Various incentives actively build and reinforce this motivation. When people feel direct, tangible outcomes from their actions, they often find the drive to continue. This "immediate sensation" mirrors the endorphin rush of a sporting achievement, receiving a highly anticipated job offer.[156]

Building sustainability starts with creating experiences that clearly show the benefits of sustainable actions. For example, people often feel an immediate sense of reward when they save resources or reduce CO_2 emissions as a result of their actions. Visuals and data that show these effects increase motivation. When teams reach their sustainability goals, they feel pride and satisfaction—emotions that fuel their willingness to continue making sustainable choices.

---

[155] Fogg, 2020.
[156] Fogg, 2020.

Example

Switching brand colours to high-contrast ones that meet accessibility requirements or creating non-human personas to embody sustainability in UX.

Another form of motivation comes from anticipating future rewards or avoiding negative consequences. This long-term incentive drives sustained effort—similar to working towards a promotion. Showing the benefits of a sustainable path for both the company and the environment strengthens motivation. Clear, achievable short-term goals that contribute to a larger vision help increase commitment.

Example

The overarching goal is to reduce the resource consumption of a digital application—such as the company's own website. To achieve this larger objective, the following individual goals guide the process: consolidating and optimising images and videos, auditing content to remove redundant information, mapping user journeys, and optimising them afterward. Each of these steps represents a short-term goal and contributes progress towards a milestone.

A sense of belonging and shared vision strongly motivates people. Our social nature drives us to seek acceptance and connection. Embedding sustainability into a company's values and culture builds this sense of collective purpose. When people identify with a vision for a more sustainable future, they feel more committed to shaping that future. Collaborative projects, discussions, and celebrations of sustainable ideas strengthen this shared identity. Highlighting teams or individuals who contribute to sustainable design reinforces the feeling of being part of a movement that makes a real difference.

In short, these motivational drivers are:

- Immediate, tangible experiences
- Long-term incentives and milestone achievements
- Community and shared values

Ability

Ability involves skill level, available time, and resources, and the ease of performing a task. When an action takes too much time or effort, people find it hard to keep it up. In this case, it helps to divide behaviour change into manageable steps. For example, starting an accessible design does not require a fully accessible application right away. A first small step could improve colour contrast or adding alternative text to images.

Education and awareness are the foundation for change. It begins with understanding and valuing the topic—from individual teams to leadership. Training programs and workshops help raise awareness and teach how to integrate sustainability into processes.

Triggers
Triggers are the final driver of action—even highly motivated individuals with the necessary skills rarely act without the right prompts. Triggers include incentives, encouragement, or timely moments that prompt action.

An incentive increases motivation when it is lacking, for example, through inspiring messages, quotes, or motivational cards. A supporter is useful when motivation is present, but the ability to act needs to be increased, for instance, through checklists for sustainability that simplifies processes. An impulse serves as a timely reminder when both motivation and ability are already high. It acts as a temporal cue, like a calendar entry that marks the end of a quarter and signals an associated deadline for sustainable change.

Example

A design review presents inspiring success stories about how accessible products have positively impacted the lives of people with disabilities. These stories actively motivate design and development teams to support accessibility (incentive). The team added a digital accessibility checklist to the workflow. It includes specific items, such as verifying contrast values or using alternative texts for images (supporter). Teams receive a recurring calendar reminder to perform an accessibility check at the end of each sprint (impulse).

Altogether, this transformation model shows that motivation, ability, and triggering structures are critical for transforming sustainability from an abstract idea into a lived company value. When leadership models these values and aligns processes accordingly, sustainability evolves from an abstract goal to an integrated part of company culture.

10.5 Summary and Conclusion

Integrating sustainability into companies and their departments is a multi-layered process that requires strategic thinking, targeted measures, and the involvement of stakeholders. A sustainable transformation is only possible through a holistic approach. It is crucial to anchor sustainability in the corporate strategies and align the company's own processes accordingly. Systematic measurement methods and clear metrics are essential for tracking progress and guiding well-informed, strategic decisions.

Sustainable change also depends on building a company-wide culture that brings shared values to life—in strategy and in everyday actions.

Embedding sustainability into company structures and in specific areas, such as user experience, depends on strategic orientation, operational measures, and cultural changes—and on how effectively these elements work together. Sustainability becomes firmly rooted in organisational practice when strategy, action, and values are aligned and mutually reinforcing.

11 SUSTAINABLE UX—CHALLENGES AND SOLUTIONS

Integrating sustainability into UX processes requires a fundamental shift in perspective. The focus expands beyond delivering an optimal user experience to include responsible use of resources, environmental protection, and inclusivity. This broader ambition introduces a range of challenges—both conceptual and practical.

This section identifies the major obstacles to sustainable user experience design and proposes actionable solutions.

11.1 Balancing Longevity and Functional Growth

"How can organisations balance the principle of longevity and digital waste reduction with the demand for continuous feature development?"

This is a legitimate and highly relevant question in today's fast-paced digital environment. Rather than yielding to the pressure to continuously expand functionality, teams can prioritise the actual needs of the target audience, assess technical feasibility, weigh costs and benefits, and consider long-term sustainability.

Some organisations still continue creating many new features from an internal perspective, but these features do not necessarily provide added value. Internal views or stakeholder requirements are not a valid basis for introducing new functions or solutions. In cases of doubt, this can lead to enormous development costs and the target group not using the feature at all or only very sporadically. The research and analysis phase is the cornerstone for recognising the essential needs and wishes of the target group. Thoughtful, data-driven feature development is key to ensuring the longevity of digital applications.

Stakeholders often approach teams with fully defined requirements and expect implementation without further evaluation. Many times, teams skip essential steps such as needs analysis, problem definition, cost-benefit evaluation, and technical feasibility assessment. Rather than integrating new functions through a structured development process, teams still tend to implement them on ad hoc basis.

To solve these challenges, the following points need to be addressed early in the process:

- **User needs and problem definition:** Evaluate whether the requested feature delivers business and/or user-centered value. Does it solve a real problem, or is it simply a "nice-to-have?" Each requirement should be based on a thorough user needs. Stakeholders must clearly and comprehensively articulate the problem the feature should solve.
- **Validation of the requirements:** Test stakeholder assumptions against data and user insights. Validating requirements at an early stage helps identify ineffective or unnecessary features and supports better prioritisation.
- **Cost-benefit analysis:** Once a feature aligns with both business goals and user needs, assess whether its benefits outweigh the associated costs or negative impacts. Traditional cost-benefit frameworks help evaluate financial, time-related, and technical resources, along with long-term implications.
- **Prioritisation within the product roadmap:** Determine whether the feature aligns with the product strategy and strengthens core functionality or supports the long-term vision. Use methods such as *RICE* (Reach, Impact, Confidence, Effort), the *Value* vs. *Complexity Quadrant*, the Kano model, or *MoSCoW* (Must have, Should have, Could have, Won't have) to support structured prioritisation.
- **Technical feasibility analysis:** Is implementation technically sound and sustainable? Will it lead to increased code complexity or maintainability issues? A technical feasibility check determines if the feature fits into the current architecture or introduces risks, such as technical debt.
- **Propose alternative solutions:** If a feature meets strategic needs but faces challenges—such as budget limitations or capacity constraints—explore alternative implementation options. Gradual improvements or phased rollouts offer flexibility while still addressing stakeholder needs and preserving valuable ideas.

These approaches help to create long-lasting, efficient solutions, reduce digital waste, and strengthen user trust in the product. A thoughtful design that includes only what is truly necessary plays a key role in advancing sustainable user experience design.

11.2 Skill-up: Requirements for Knowledge and Skills

Design today is multifaceted. The field of user experience constantly demands new skills and competencies from professionals. Besides a deep understanding of user-centered design and prototyping tools, professionals must also work in interdisciplinary teams and be familiar with agile methods like *Scrum* (a framework based on time-boxed development sprints and defined roles) or *Kanban* (a visual system for managing workflow and continuous delivery). The ability to analyse data and incorporate feedback into design decisions is just as important as an awareness of current design trends and accessibility. Soft skills such as empathy, strong communication, and problem-solving ability to complete the profile.

Current design methods and approaches often lack the awareness of the profound impact that design and development have on our world. Design shapes everything that surrounds us. In fact, according to Norman, design is the driving force behind many of the current challenges we face.[157] To positively shape the impact on our environment, the view of design must change. Designers need to shift their perspective—towards a more conscious approach to the power they possess.

This further expands the expectations placed on designers. The field of user experience represents the interests of the target audience, stakeholders, and the company, but also assumes responsibility for wider impacts. Designers must be able to reconcile these concerns and understand that every decision influences users, business outcomes, and society.

The skills requirements mentioned above can be supplemented with knowledge of:

- Sustainability management
- Economics
- Business management
- Technologies
- Humanities and ethics
- History
- Politics

The growing complexity of knowledge challenges teams to rethink how they structure roles. Instead of expecting one person to master every skill equally, companies benefit from focusing on individual disciplines. The shift is already reflected in specialised fields such as UX research, architecture, engineering, and writing.

Education plays a crucial role by building the foundation for both hard and soft skills. It shapes the basis for continuous learning and future development. While topics like business and ethics hold a firm place in many curricula, sustainability, and environmental impact still receive little attention—if they appear at all.

11.3 Appealing by Design: Challenges in Sustainable UX

Taking sustainability into account often involves *compromises* between aesthetic appeal and environmentally responsible design choices. Users expect visually rich, interactive, and high-quality designs that enhance the experience. Simultaneously, elaborate graphics, animations, and data-heavy content increase energy consumption and conflict with sustainability goals.

One clear example lies in the use and optimisation of digital media. Visually striking elements—such as large images, videos, or animations—create strong visual impact but also lead to longer loading times, greater data transfer, and

[157] Norman, 2023.

higher server energy use. Reducing image sizes, eliminating unnecessary animations, and writing efficient code help lower digital weight without significantly affecting the user experience.

Dark mode design introduces a similar trade-off. While not every interface benefits in appearance or usability from darker themes, dark mode reduces energy consumption on OLED displays. In these cases, designers face the challenge of maintaining visual appeal while reducing environmental impact—for example, by combining bright design with minimal interactive elements.

Sustainable UX goes beyond energy efficiency. It also includes long-term usability and accessibility. A design that remains functional across years and devices supports sustainability by reducing the need for redesigns or replacements. Inclusive design adds further complexity: it requires deliberate choices in colour, typography, and animation. Elements like parallax scrolling or rapid visual effects may overwhelm users with cognitive disabilities or sensory sensitivities and should be used with caution.

Branding decisions often create additional hurdles. When brand colours offer poor contrast or lack accessibility considerations, integrating them into a sustainable design becomes increasingly difficult. The same applies to typography—delicate fonts, thin line weights, or confusing character shapes (such as lowercase "l" and uppercase "I") reduce readability and increase development effort unnecessarily.

11.4 Summary and Conclusion

Sustainable user experience requires a holistic rethink that goes far beyond a narrow focus on usability. Challenges—such as balancing innovation with longevity, bridging interdisciplinary skill sets, or reconciling aesthetic expectations with sustainability requirements—become manageable through systematic approaches, clear prioritisation, and a strong awareness of the impact of design decisions.

The future of sustainable user experience lies in an interplay of data-based decisions, specialised collaboration, and training—focusing clearly on a sense of responsibility and resource-saving innovation.

12 SUSTAINABILITY VS. REGENERATION–THE LIMITS OF SUSTAINABLE UX

In today's discussion about sustainable design, there is growing recognition that sustainability alone is not enough to solve complex ecological and social challenges. A pure focus on preserving what still exists cannot repair the damage that has already been done. Our way of life has already caused irreparable destruction. To move forward, the goal needs to extend beyond maintaining the status quo toward regeneration–a design approach that actively restores ecosystems and prevents further damage to the planet.

Rethinking sustainability means recognising the responsibility to give back more than we take. This shift requires a deeper understanding of our role in the world and a shift towards a positive, regenerative impact on our planet.

> *"While concerns of sustainability and ethics bear closely on this work, ultimately regenerative UX extends beyond the problem of controlling for negative societal or environmental consequences. The term ›regenerative‹ promises renewal and rebirth, not merely the mitigation of harms."*
>
> (Wright 2022, p. 115)

12.1 Regenerative Approaches

Profit-oriented organisations increasingly explore models that embed regenerative principles as alternatives to purely profit-driven practices. Pioneers like Carol Sanford describe a "regenerative economy" as a direct response to systems that have long harmed ecosystems and cultures.[158] Sanford emphasises the need for inner transformation–shifts that connect individuals and organisations to deeper meaning and purpose. Through this lens, businesses adopt practices that foster long-term resilience and vitality.

Roland and Landua[159], along with Lyle[160], expand this view by highlighting regenerative strategies that address both ecological and economic renewal, and also the cultivation of diverse forms of capital–social, cultural, and ecological. These approaches rely on natural cycles and principles such as circularity, energy flow, and integrating ecosystem functions to move beyond

[158] Sanford, 2017.
[159] Roland & Landua, 2015.
[160] Lyle, 1996.

conservation and actively regenerate resources. Their focus lies on building holistic systems that support long-term sustainability while deepening the connections among companies, communities, and the living world.

12.2 Regenerative Approaches in User Experience Design

While sustainable user experience addresses critical concerns such as climate, ethics, diversity, value creation, and user trust, a regenerative approach goes further. It seeks to avoid harm, and to restore and enhance systems—drawing inspiration from nature's capacity to renew itself. This perspective expands the scope of design and opens alternative paths for innovation.

Companies and design teams take an active role in advancing regenerative practices and reducing environmental impact through intentional actions, including:

- **Developing regenerative digital systems**: Designing digital products and platforms that support resource-efficient production and influence user behaviour toward regenerative outcomes.
- **Educating and raising awareness**: Clearly communicating energy use and emissions empowers users to make informed choices that align with regenerative principles.
- **Promotion of repair and recycling processes**: Integrating functions that make repair and recycling options visible and accessible contributes to a circular economy and supports regenerative practices.
- **Creating immersive and regenerative experiences**: Digital experiences that focus on nature and the environment raise awareness of ecological challenges and bring regenerative principles to life.
- **Promoting community participation and collaboration**: Platforms that enable shared initiatives and cooperative efforts reinforce local networks and amplify collective impact, such as through crowd action projects.

Although the regeneration approach in user experience remains at an early stage, it holds significant potential. Many companies and design teams already lay the foundations by integrating sustainable practices into their processes—creating a solid base for regenerative design to evolve and expand.

12.3 Summary and Conclusion

Sustainable user experience reaches its limits when it focuses primarily on conserving existing resources. While this is a crucial step, it fails to repair the ecological and social damage that has already been done. The current situation demands a more ambitious approach—one that minimises harm and actively restores and strengthens systems. Companies and design teams need to move beyond conventional sustainability and develop models that foster long-term resilience and deliver positive environmental, social, and economic outcomes.

Regenerative approaches within the corporate context are based on principles such as a circular economy, raising awareness, promoting repair and recycling, and creating immersive experiences that reconnect people with nature and the environment.

Although the regenerative approach in user experience design remains in its early stages, it holds significant promise. Companies and design teams play a key role in driving this evolution by building on sustainable practices and expanding them through regenerative thinking. This shift lays the groundwork for lasting, positive impact on the environment, society, and the economy.

13 ARTIFICIAL INTELLIGENCE AND UX–PROGRESS OR SUSTAINABILITY TRAP?

At a digital sustainability event in Frankfurt last year, I spoke with a participant about the future of user experience design. During our conversation, he asked what happens when applications begin adapting in real time to people's lives—shaping themselves dynamically around user behaviour. What does this shift mean for UX when a contextual search becomes the entry point of a shopping journey, and the interface builds itself only as needed? Will we continue to design digital products the way we do today, or will experiences begin with a minimalist search bar, unfolding adaptively based on user intent?

When my 15-year-old son searches for clothes online, he doesn't browse through online shops or navigate menus. He enters keywords directly into a search engine and expects instant, visually driven results tailored to his preferences. For him, speed and relevance matter most. Is this efficiency-driven, hyper-personalised model becoming the foundation of future UX?

Yet, other scenarios tell a different story—those who enjoy browsing full collections, taking their time with discovery, and finding by chance rather than intention. For these users, the experience itself holds value. Inspiration and the joy of discovery are more important than efficiency or quick results.

Artificial intelligence holds transformative potential for UX. Thoughtful integration supports more responsive workflows and tailored, real-time interactions that align with diverse user expectations. However, this progress introduces real risks. Ethical concerns around data privacy, algorithmic bias, and long-term sustainability require more than technical fixes—they demand intentional design and continuous reflection. Without this, AI-enhanced UX may shift from innovation to trap.

13.1 Artificial Intelligence and UX: A Smart Match?

Designing efficient and aesthetically pleasing user experiences is now one of the most critical factors in the success of digital products. The rise of artificial intelligence is opening entirely new doors for optimising UX processes and tailoring designs even more effectively to user needs. AI already plays a vital role in UX, helping teams automate repetitive tasks and providing deeper insights into user behaviour and expectations—as well as environmental impacts. With intelligent analytics tools, personalised approaches, and proactive support, AI is changing both the landscape of the digital world and the way we design experiences. AI's role in today's UX teams:

- **Idea generation and brainstorming:** AI is useful for creating concepts and design suggestions. It offers creative impulses, initiates discussions, and delivers concrete suggestions for processes or content.
- **Data analysis and understanding target audience:** Using AI, we quickly process large datasets, revealing behavioural patterns, user trends, and hidden correlations to teams.
- **Prototyping and design automation:** AI streamlines prototyping by generating layout suggestions or automatically adjusting existing designs, accelerating workflows and freeing up time for creative strategy.
- **Usability testing and feedback evaluation:** Tools based on AI, such as modern heat maps, eye-tracking software, and automated sentiment analysis, evaluate interactions in real time and interpret results for improved decision-making.

Proactive and Predictive Approaches

As already mentioned, AI can proactively identify problems and recommend preventative solutions to minimise user frustration. Even more promising are predictive capabilities that anticipate user needs, preferences, or market trends by analysing historical data patterns.

Proactive vs. Predictive

Proactive approaches act before a problem arises—offering preventive assistance or notifications based on anticipated behaviour.
Predictive methods use data analysis to accurately forecast user needs, thus creating intelligent and seamless anticipatory designs.

Together, these applications allow UX teams to craft more personalised, responsive, and context-aware digital experiences. AI, when used responsibly, strengthens both user satisfaction and operational efficiency.

13.2 Using AI to Create Individual Experiences

As early as 1993, Don Peppers and Martha Rogers outlined a fundamental shift in marketing in their influential book *"The One to One Future."*[161] They predicted the demise of "cold marketing" and emphasised the growing need for personalisation. That revolutionary idea has since become one of the greatest challenges for companies and marketing teams.

Hyperpersonalisation

The concept of personalisation, as introduced by Peppers and Rogers, goes well

[161] Peppers & Rogers, 1993.

beyond general approaches. It is about placing individuals at the center and responding specifically to their needs. While traditional personalisation is typically based on segmented target groups and basic user data, we have now reached an era where a new standard is emerging: hyperpersonalisation.

Hyperpersonalisation

Hyperpersonalisation exceeds regular personalisation by providing customised experiences that are specific to the unique behaviours, circumstances, and needs of each individual. The aim is to create relevant, meaningful interactions that foster trust and strengthen long-term customer relationships.

AI-powered recommendation engines provide a practical example of adaptive, user-centered technology. These systems suggest products while also adapting dynamically to the user's context. Product recommendations shift based on variables such as time of day, location, or even inferred mood. For instance, an online shop promotes coffee in the morning and highlights calming teas in the evening. Content evolves in response to prior interactions, resulting in a seamless and personalised experience.

Adaptive Interfaces

While hyperpersonalisation tailors content, features, and offers based on user behaviour and preferences, adaptive interfaces adjust digital environments dynamically in response to interactions and contextual factors. This includes modifying layouts, navigation, or even platform functionality to better align with the user's current situation.

Imagine a user named Karl searching for a new outfit. He visits an AI-powered fashion online shop and begins his journey:

- **Contextual input**: Karl types: "blue sweater, brown pants, matching shoes." The AI processes his request along with previous purchases, preferred brands, real-time availability, and current trends.
- **Dynamic product selection**: The system presents clothing items that match Karl's style and colour preferences based on the query.
- **Personalised filtering**: Relevant filter options appear—such as price range or brand—alongside complementary suggestions like outerwear, tailored to Karl's browsing habits.
- **Virtual try-on**: A visualisation tool displays how the outfit looks on Karl, using either an uploaded photo or a digital avatar.
- **Live AI assistance**: A chatbot provides support, for instance, by offering vegan footwear as an alternative to leather options.

Challenges and Conclusion

While hyperpersonalisation and adaptive interfaces offer substantial potential, their implementation involves several key challenges:

- **Data privacy and ethics:** Managing large volumes of personal data requires strict adherence to data protection standards. Transparency and compliance with privacy regulations remain non-negotiable.
- **Technological complexity:** These systems operate on advanced algorithms and real-time processing, demanding considerable investment in infrastructure and specialised talent.
- **Data integration and quality**: CRM systems, real-time interactions, and external platforms must provide unified and reliable information. Inconsistent or low-quality data reduces system effectiveness.
- **Real-time responsiveness:** Timely and precise adaptations are essential. Delays or mismatches negatively impact the user experience.
- **User acceptance and transparency:** Overpersonalisation or opaque system behaviour risks alienating users. Maintaining a clear balance between automation and user control is vital.
- **Accessibility and inclusivity:** Adaptive systems must remain functional and intuitive for users with diverse needs and abilities.
- **Contextual relevance:** Personalisation must align with the user's current context. Irrelevant or intrusive suggestions erode trust and reduce engagement.
- **Resource costs:** Developing and maintaining these systems involves substantial human and financial investment. Clear strategic priorities are necessary to ensure meaningful returns.

The challenge for companies is to adopt these technologies strategically, aligning them with business goals and user needs. Hyperpersonalisation and adaptive interfaces depend on powerful algorithms and high-quality data. Used wisely and ethically, they help companies build deeper customer relationships, improve satisfaction, and ensure long-term competitiveness.

13.3 AI Act: Preserving Ethics and Transparency

Artificial intelligence continues to advance rapidly and now influences many aspects of daily life—from medicine and business to mobility and communication. This rapid development also brings important ethical questions to the forefront: How do we ensure responsible development and the use of AI systems? What rights and responsibilities must companies and individuals uphold when engaging with AI? And how do we prevent misuse that undermines human dignity, justice, and transparency?

To address these concerns, the European Union introduced the AI Act, establishing a legal framework that promotes safe and ethical AI use across Europe.[162] The regulation seeks to reduce risks while fostering innovation. It outlines clear requirements for developing, testing, and monitoring AI systems to align with the EU's core values, particularly human rights, data protection,

---

[162] European Parliament & Council of the European Union., 2024.

and ethical principles.

The AI Act will shape the way designers create user experiences. High-risk applications must provide transparency, visibility, and clarity—requiring designers to clearly explain how AI systems work and how they reach decisions.

Risk-Based Classification of AI Systems

The AI Act defines four categories of risk; each associated with different requirements:

- **Unacceptable risk**: AI systems that present a clear threat to individuals' rights and safety are prohibited. This includes practices such as social scoring, which assess and influence behaviour to control or manipulate individuals.
- **High risk**: AI applications classified as high risk—those that impact people's safety or fundamental rights—must meet strict requirements. This category includes systems used in healthcare (e.g. medical diagnostics), mobility (e.g. autonomous driving), and employment (e.g. automated hiring). These systems undergo rigorous documentation, continuous monitoring, and regular compliance checks.
- **Limited risk**: These systems remain permitted but must comply with specific transparency requirements. For example, recommendation systems must inform users that AI is involved and clearly explain why specific suggestions appear when suggesting products or media content.
- **Minimal or low risk**: AI applications with negligible impact—such as those used for system maintenance or performance optimisation—fall outside the scope of significant regulation under the AI Act.

Conclusion

The European Union's AI Act represents a major step toward the responsible and transparent use of artificial intelligence. It aims to balance technological innovation with ethical integrity and societal values. In user experience, the Act underscores the need for human-centered design—placing transparency, traceability, and fairness at the core. UX professionals must harness AI's potential while critically assessing and guiding its application to ensure it supports user rights and expectations.

13.4 AI and its Ecological Impact

Machine learning and automated processes personalise digital interfaces, optimise workflows, and solve complex tasks in real time. These capabilities sound revolutionary. Yet, they prompt a critical question: how does artificial intelligence align with sustainability? Does this technology support responsible resource use—or conflict with it?

Training and running large language models—like those behind many AI systems—demands enormous computing power and energy. As a result, AI contributes significantly to the ecological footprint of digital infrastructure.

Simultaneously, AI holds potential to actively support sustainability. Intelligent systems enhance resource efficiency, streamline supply chains, and accelerate the development of renewable energy solutions. These dual impacts call for closer examination: do AI and sustainability reinforce one another, or do they stand at odds?

Resource Consumption and Carbon Emissions

According to a 2024 study by the Electric Power Research Institute (EPRI), a single prompt submitted to a text-based AI like ChatGPT consumes about ten times more energy than a Google search.[163] With the number of monthly active ChatGPT users doubling within a year, energy demands are growing rapidly.

The training phase of large AI models consumes particularly high amounts of energy. For example, training GPT-3 alone generated about 552 tons of CO_2—comparable to the annual emissions of over 100 average cars.[164]

Question 1: Does the increased efficiency of AI justify its ecological footprint?

One hypothesis suggests that AI improves efficiency enough to save more resources than it consumes. For instance, AI-powered search tools reduce the number of redundant or inefficient queries, which lowers the overall volume of data processing. Despite this potential, reliable evidence remains limited. A meaningful analysis must compare AI's direct energy consumption with the indirect savings that result from enhanced user efficiency.

Question 2: What strategies can reduce AI's energy consumption?

Advancing algorithms and hardware plays a critical role. Purpose-built components, such as Tensor Processing Units (TPUs) process tasks more efficiently. Running data centers on renewable energy further reduces environmental impact. already operate parts of their infrastructure in a climate-neutral way, demonstrating that scalable solutions exist.

Question 3: How can AI be applied responsibly in UX design?

Responsible AI use in UX depends on conscious and selective application, guided by sustainability principles. Everyone involved in the development process must evaluate each use case critically and ask:

- Does the task involve enough complexity to use AI?
- Would a manual solution deliver similar results with reasonable effort?
- Does AI generate meaningful insights or noticeably improve quality?
- Does the solution match the task in scope and efficiency?
- Do smaller models or edge computing options suit the context better?

[163] Electric Power Research Institute (EPRI), 2024.
[164] Saenko, 2024.

- Do existing data sources support the task without extra processing??

Answering these questions helps prevent unnecessary AI implementation and ensures the design process minimises resource use.

Conclusion

AI offers powerful opportunities but also introduces significant responsibilities. The rising energy demands of large models place considerable pressure on environmental resources. While AI often increases efficiency and drives innovation, every application requires critical evaluation, especially considering its ecological consequences.

Integrating AI responsibly means focusing on purposeful use, ongoing assessment, and ethical alignment. Using AI simply because it is available does not justify its deployment. Responsible practice in UX—and beyond—requires a careful balance between technological advancement, environmental sustainability, and social accountability.

13.5 Can Artificial Intelligence Jeopardise Jobs in UX?

Jakob Nielsen's statement, *"You're not going to lose your job to AI – but you will lose your job to somebody who uses AI if you do not."*[165] aptly captures the potential impact of artificial intelligence on the UX profession.

AI already boosts productivity by automating repetitive tasks, generating design prototypes quickly, and analysing user behaviour data with precision. Within just five years, professionals are expected to complete twice as much work simultaneously by leveraging AI. This shift changes the professional dynamic: AI does not replace UX professionals, but those who adopt AI tools outperform those who resist them.

Professionals who integrate AI into their workflows gain more time for strategic and creative tasks—such as shaping innovative experiences and deepening human-digital interactions. As this shift continues, companies will prioritise individuals who use AI effectively, recognising the greater value delivered through efficiency and insight.

13.6 Summary and Conclusion

Artificial intelligence can enhance user experience by increasing efficiency, personalisation, and adaptability in digital applications. Integrated thoughtfully, AI empowers UX teams to automate routine tasks, process large datasets rapidly, and design predictive, user-centered solutions. These capabilities boost productivity and unlock new potential for innovation and personalised services.

This progress also brings challenges—especially regarding data protection, ethical accountability, and sustainability. The European Union's AI Act reflects

[165] Nielsen (cited in Stevens, 2023).

a growing commitment to responsible, transparent AI. This regulatory framework requires high-risk AI systems to align with fundamental societal values, including human rights, fairness, and non-discrimination. For UX professionals, this means ensuring that AI-driven systems remain explainable, traceable, and free of bias.

One of the most urgent concerns involves AI's high energy demands. While intelligent systems help reduce resource waste through targeted processes and streamlined workflows, training and operating large models consume vast amounts of energy. This creates a paradox: AI supports sustainability in some contexts but undermines it in others, depending on its implementation.

The societal impact of AI remains complex. AI simplifies workflows, removes barriers, and strengthens engagement. Yet it also carries risks—amplifying bias, reinforcing echo chambers, and diminishing user agency. Without strong governance, organisations lose visibility and control, increasing the likelihood of unintended harm.

To apply AI ethically and sustainably in UX, teams across disciplines must commit to clear priorities. This involves establishing and following ethical standards, designing AI systems with transparency while minimising resource consumption, and ensuring data privacy along with user autonomy. It also requires fostering inclusive and accessible design practices, and maintaining a thoughtful balance between technological innovation and both human and environmental wellbeing.

Ultimately, the goal is not to use AI simply because it exists—but to apply it in ways that deliver real, responsible, and inclusive value.

14 SUMMARY OF THE BOOK

Driven by both societal change and regulatory developments, sustainability has become a central pillar of modern business practices. It is now a decisive factor for the long-term success and public acceptance of companies and their products.

The growing importance of sustainability stems not only from ethical responsibility but also from economic and technological necessity. In user experience, this shift requires teams to apply standards that integrate usability, efficiency, and environmental awareness. Sustainable design principles reduce environmental impact while enhancing the quality of user interactions.

Applying these principles generates value for both society and business. From a societal perspective, sustainable design promotes ecological awareness and long-term well-being. On the corporate side, it strengthens brand image and deepens emotional connections with target audiences. Companies are responsible for actively managing and reducing the environmental footprint of their products and services. A well-designed user experience supports this effort by increasing the acceptance of sustainable offerings. When users engage with intuitive and accessible solutions, they more readily adopt sustainable behaviours.

Behavioural design, green defaults, and green nudging subtly empower users to make sustainable choices. These strategies avoid pressure and instead make sustainability feel effortless. Sustainable UX involves three interrelated dimensions: ecological, social, and economic. This framework ensures digital products remain environmentally responsible, socially inclusive, and economically viable. Design principles like minimalism, longevity focused design, and calm design focus on reducing resource use while keeping user needs at the center of the design process.

Sustainable UX influences the full lifecycle of a product—from user research and data collection to design, implementation, and testing. Practices such as paperless collaboration, green hosting, and energy-efficient interaction patterns help reduce the digital footprint. Digital accessibility also plays a key role, ensuring that services reach everyone, regardless of ability. Following standards like the Web Content Accessibility Guidelines (WCAG) supports both inclusion and long-term usability.

Success depends on strong leadership and a design culture that prioritises sustainability. Cross-functional collaboration, clear goal-setting, and transparent communication reinforce sustainable practices. While some challenges persist—such as organisational gaps or missing skills—training and awareness campaigns help close these gaps and build momentum.

Despite progress, sustainable UX still faces limitations—especially in moving toward regenerative design approaches that restore and renew social and environmental systems. Artificial intelligence and automation support this transition by enabling smarter, data-driven processes. Their use, however, requires clear justification based on resource savings and long-term impact.

Artificial intelligence continues to shape both society and the UX field. It supports personalisation, accelerates design processes, and contributes to sustainable innovation. However, its high energy consumption requires scrutiny. Rather than replacing human creativity or decision-making, AI complements design efforts and strengthens outcomes. When applied purposefully, artificial intelligence can enrich user experience and support the transition to a more sustainable digital future.

15 RECOMMENDED ACTIONS

This final chapter outlines concrete strategies for embedding sustainability principles into design processes and corporate strategy. These actionable insights, drawn from the book's core findings, are intended to help teams and organisations integrate sustainability into their digital products and operational culture.

15.1 Recommended Actions for Designers

The following design-specific recommendations summarise essential principles for creating sustainable digital products. The aim is to incorporate sustainability early in the design process, establish user-centered and resource-efficient standards, and foster inclusive, energy-conscious solutions.

Integrate Sustainability Principles Into the Design Process

- Embed approaches such as minimalist design, calm design, and design for longevity to reduce environmental impact
- Audit designs regularly to eliminate unnecessary elements that increase energy use or complexity
- Develop user-centered, sustainable design standards
- Structure journeys that actively support sustainable behaviour by making environmentally friendly choices more visible and rewarding
- Apply green nudging to integrate sustainability into UX naturally
- Reinforce positive behaviour through consistent, encouraging feedback

Implement Energy-Efficient Interactions and Technologies

- Optimise UI interactions and use green hosting services to minimise energy consumption
- Choose alternatives, such as paperless workflows and eco-friendly prototyping tools

Ensure Accessibility and Inclusion

- Design digital products to meet WCAG and international accessibility standards
- Focus on simple, inclusive interfaces that expand access to all users

Treat sustainable design as a foundational principle, not an optional add-on!

15.2 Recommended Actions for Management

The following actions focus on leadership and organisational practices that embed sustainability into culture, operations, and strategy. Effective implementation depends on clear goals, interdisciplinary collaboration, transparency, and openness to change.

Establish Sustainability a Core Company Value

- Define measurable sustainability goals and align them with the company's mission and vision
- Communicate how individual roles contribute to these goals to build shared responsibility

Promote Interdisciplinary Collaboration

- Facilitate collaboration between UX, development, product management, marketing, and other teams
- Create recurring opportunities for cross-departmental exchange of sustainable practices

Provide Training and Resources for Sustainable UX

- Offer trainings and workshops on sustainable design, behavioural psychology, accessibility, and green technologies
- Equip teams with tools, templates, and frameworks that simplify sustainable implementation

Establish Monitoring and Evaluation of Sustainability Goals

- Track environmental and resource impact of digital projects through defined metrics
- Conduct regular audits to assess progress and identify areas for improvement

Foster Communication and Transparency

- Share sustainability updates regularly and celebrate UX-related achievements
- Involve teams in green initiatives and communicate success stories internally and externally

Evaluate Emerging Technologies for Sustainability Potential

- Apply AI and automation selectively to improve efficiency and reduce waste
- Assess new technologies continuously to ensure alignment with long-term sustainability goals
- Invest in innovation that supports resource-conscious and responsible product development

16 CHAPTER OVERVIEW

This chapter offers a structured overview of each chapter in the book, serving as a quick reference for the main themes and insights presented throughout the book.

Chapter 1: Sustainability—A Historical Overview

Provides a historical overview of sustainability, outlining major global milestones such as the Brundtland Report and the UN's Sustainable Development Goals. It also introduces key business frameworks like the triple bottom line, ESG criteria, and recent digital sustainability standards, such as the Sustainable Web Manifesto.

Chapter 2: How Do User Experience and Sustainability fit Together?

Establishes the conceptual foundation linking sustainability and UX. It explains the evolution from usability and user-centered design to life-centered design, emphasising the need to consider environmental and societal impacts in digital product development.

Chapter 3: Why Sustainability Is Essential for Companies and Society

Outlines why sustainability is essential both for society and for businesses. The chapter explores the environmental impact of the digital industry and presents sustainability as both a moral responsibility and a strategic advantage for companies. By addressing the ecological footprint of digital products and services, the chapter highlights how sustainable practices enhance corporate reputation, drive innovation, and help attract and retain talent.

Chapter 4: How User Experience Affects the Target Audience

Analyses the influence of UX on user perception and behaviour. Compares traditional UX with sustainability-driven UX, demonstrating how ethical, inclusive, and transparent design fosters trust and emotional connection.

Chapter 5: How Can We Raise Awareness of Sustainability?

Explores strategies for raising awareness through design. Drawing on behavioural science, the chapter introduces methods such as behavioural design, green nudging, and storytelling, emphasising ethical and inclusive application.

Chapter 6: The Three Pillars of Sustainable UX: People, Planet, and Profit

Outlines the ecological, social, and economic pillars of sustainable UX. Examines how each dimension influences design choices—from energy-efficient interactions to social inclusivity and financial resilience.

Chapter 7: Sustainable Design Principles

Presents actionable design principles, including Sustainable by Design, Slow UX, Minimalist Design, and Design for Longevity, Mobile-First, and Calm Design. Emphasises combining these approaches to create low-impact, thoughtful digital experiences.

Chapter 8: Sustainable UX in Practice

Focuses on real-world application across UX phases—from user research to implementation. Covers tools like personas, empathy maps, and green hosting, along with media and interface optimisation strategies.

Chapter 9: Digital Accessibility and Inclusion

Addresses digital participation and accessibility, positioning them as integral to sustainable UX. It outlines legal standards like the WCAG and German regulations, while also advocating for inclusive language, easy, and plain language, and designs that reflect user diversity.

Chapter 10: Management Approaches for Sustainable UX

Shifts the focus to organisational integration and presents strategies for embedding sustainability into company structures, leadership, and culture. This chapter also highlights the role of metrics, interdisciplinary collaboration, and shared responsibility between teams and management.

Chapter 11: Sustainable UX—Challenges and Solutions

Explores the challenges in achieving sustainable UX, including balancing longevity with innovation, adapting skills, and overcoming aesthetic limitations. The chapter provides practical guidance for addressing these challenges within organisational and creative workflows.

Chapter 12: Sustainability vs. Regeneration—The Limits of Sustainable UX

Expands the conversation beyond sustainability by introducing regenerative design. Describes how digital solutions support ecosystem restoration and enhance social and environmental conditions.

Chapter 13: Artificial Intelligence and UX—Progress or Sustainability Trap?

Critically examines AI's role in UX. Explores its potential to improve personalisation and efficiency, while also addressing risks related to ecological costs, ethical transparency, hyperpersonalisation, and workforce disruption.

KEEP THIS BOOK CIRCULAR

As a responsible prosumer, you now steward the paper resources of this book. Here are a few tips on how to keep the book circular.[166]

Maintain and repair

- See wikihow.com/Repair-a-Paperback-Book for ways to:
- Clean the book
- Insert loose pages
- Repair torn pages
- Reattach a cover
- Fix the binding

Just make sure you use environmentally friendly craft glue, ones with low VOC (volatile organic compounds), are petrochemical free, and/or water-based.

Don't want to keep it anymore?

- Pass the book on to someone who can use it:
- A friend
- A school
- Drop it in at a local library
- Pop it in a street library box

Can't give it away?

Paperbacks can generally be recycled, so check your local rules to make sure you can drop it in the paper recycling bin.

[166] This circular advice page is an initiative from the Life-centred Design Lab at lifecentred.design.

REFERENCES

Adidas AG. (2022). *Adidas Annual Report 2021.* Retrieved June 2025, from https://www.adidas-group.com/

Adidas AG. (2023). *Geschäftsbericht 2022 mit Konzernabschluss und zusammengefasstem Lagebericht für die adidas AG und den Konzern zum 31. Dezember 2022.* Retrieved June 2025, from https://www.adidas-group.com/

Agenda 21. (1992). *AGENDA 21 Konferenz der Vereinten Nationen für Umwelt und Entwicklung.* Retrieved June 2025, from https://www.un.org/Depts/german/conf/agenda21/agenda_21.pdf

Aktion Mensch e.V. (2023). *Testbericht: So barrierefrei sind Online-Shops in Deutschland.* Retrieved June 2025, from https://aktion-mensch.stylelabs.cloud/api/public/content/aktion-mensch-testbericht-onlineshops_062023.pdf

Aleman, A., Wang, M., & Schaeffel, F. (2018). *Reading and Myopia: Contrast Polarity Matters.* Retrieved June 2025, from Scientific Reports 8: https://10.1038/s41598-018-28904-x

Ameseder, C. E.-H. (2017). *Die Wirkung von Storytelling in der Wissenschafts-PR.* (C. S. Christoph, Hrsg.) Wiesbaden: Springer VS.

Andersen, M. (2021). *Improve your SEO ranking by making your website environmentallyfriendly.* Retrieved June 2025, from https://sustainablewww.com/improve-your-seo-ranking-by-making-your-website-environmentally-friendly/

Barnhill, A. (2014). What is manipulation? In C. Coons, & M. Weber, *Manipulation: Theory and Practice* (pp. 51-72). Oxford University Press.

Basak, A., & Roy, S. T. (2022). *International Design Conference – Design 2022.* Retrieved June 2025, from Visual Ergonomics for Colourblindness: Applying Universal Design Principles in Graphical User Interface to Provide Affordance to the Colourblind Users.: https://www.cambridge.org/core/services/aop-cambridge-core/content/view/328DFE96A747CFF90780EDE4323D0946/S2732527X22002085a.pdf/div-class-title-visual-ergonomics-for-colourblindness-applying-universal-design-principles-in-graphical-user-interface-to-provi

Becker-Olsen, K., & Potucek, S. (2013). *Greenwashing.* (S. O. Idowu, Capaldi, N., L. Zu, & A. D. Gupta, Eds.) Berlin, Heidelberg: Springer.

Bertoldi, P., Avgerinou, M., & Castellazzi, L. (2017). *JRC Technical Reports.* Retrieved June 2025, from Trends in data centre energy consumption under the European Code of Conduct for Data Centre Energy Efficiency.: https://publications.jrc.ec.europa.eu/repository/handle/JRC108354

Bitkom e.V. (2022). *Rechenzentren in Deutschland Aktuelle Marktentwicklungen, Stand 2022.* Retrieved June 2025, from https://www.bitkom.org/sites/main/files/2022-02/10.02.22-studie-rechenzentren.pdf

Bitkom e.V. (2024). *Rechenzentren in Deutschland.* Retrieved from https://www.bitkom.org/sites/main/files/2024-11/241121-PK-Bitkom-Charts-Rechenzentren-2024-final.pdf

Bley, S., Wiethe-Körprich, M., & Weber, S. (2015). Formen kognitiver Belastung bei der Bewältigung technologiebasierter authentischer Testaufgaben – eine Validierungsstudie zur Abbildung von - beruflicher Kompetenz. *Zeitschrift für Berufs- und Wirtschaftspädagogik*(111), pp. 268-294. Retrieved from Zeitschrift für Berufs- und Wirtschaftspädagogik.

BMUV. (2015). *Übereinkommen von Paris.* Retrieved June 2025, from Bundesministerium für Umwelt, Naturschutz, nukleare Sicherheit und Verbraucherschutz: https://www.bmuv.de/fileadmin/Daten_BMU/Download_PDF/Klimaschutz/paris_abkommen_bf.pdf

Bommert, W. (2017). Klimawandel und Ernährung: „Der Druck im Kessel steigt“. (F. Mühleib, Interviewer, & Tellerrand, Editor) Retrieved from Klimawandel und Ernährung: „Der Druck im Kessel steigt“: https://institut-fuer-welternaehrung.org/klimawandel-und-ernaehrung-der-druck-im-kessel-steigt

Brandstädter, S. (2019). *Interdisziplinär erfolgreich – Modellierung, Validierung und Förderung interdisziplinärer Handlungskompetenz (Dissertation).* Retrieved June 2025, from Universität Heidelberg: https://archiv.ub.uni-heidelberg.de/volltextserver/29256/1/Brandstädter_Interdisziplinär Erfolgreich.pdf

Bredel, U., & Maas, C. (2018). *Leichte Sprache. Handbuch Barrierefreie Kommunikation.* (C. Maas, & I. Rink, Eds.) Frank & Timme Verlag GmbH.

Brosch, N., & Schauerte, P. (2023). *Nachhaltigkeit aus Kapitalmarktsicht: Transparenz bei ESG-Daten treibt Nachhaltigkeit voran.* Retrieved June 2025, from https://www.haufe.de/controlling/controllerpraxis/kapitalmarkt-sieht-transparenz-als-nachhaltigkeitstreiber_112_601490.html

Brown, T. (2019). *Change By Design. Revised and Updated.* New York: HarperCollins.

Brundtland, G. H. (1987). *Our Common Future: Report of the World Commission on Environment and Development.* Geneva: UN-Dokument A/42/427.

Bundesregierung. (2021). *Deutsche Nachhaltigkeitsstrategie – Weiterentwicklung 2021 (Kurzfassung).* Retrieved June 2025, from https://www.bundesregierung.de/resource/blob/975274/1873516/9d73d857a3f7f0f8df5ac1b4c349fa07/2021-03-10-dns-2021-finale-langfassung-barrierefrei-data.pdf

Burtscher, L., Barret, D., Borkar, A., Grinberg, V., Jahnke, K., Kendrew, S., . . . McCaughrean, M. J. (2020). *The carbon footprint of large astronomy meetings.* Retrieved June 2025, from https://doi.org/10.1038/s41550-020-1207-z

Business Wire. (2021). *Recent study reveals more than a third of global consumers are willing to pay more for sustainability as demand grows for environmentally-friendly alternatives*. Retrieved June 2025, from https://www.businesswire.com/news/home/20211014005090/en/Recent-Study-Reveals-More-Than-a-Third-of-Global-Consumers-Are-Willing-to-Pay-More-for-Sustainability-as-Demand-Grows-for-Environmentally-Friendly-Alternatives

Campaign Live. (2016). *Brands, not government, drive social change, say consumers – study*. Retrieved June 2025, from https://www.campaignlive.co.uk/article/brands-not-government-drive-social-change-say-consumers-study/1380448

Capgemini Research Institute. (2023). *Consumer Trends Studie 2023: Was für den Verbraucher von heute zählt*. Retrieved June 2025, from https://www.capgemini.com/de-de/insights/research/what-matters-to-todays-consumer-2023/

Capgemini Researh Institute. (2020). *Wie Nachhaltigkeit die Konsumgewohnheiten grundlegend verändert.* Retrieved June 2025, from https://www.capgemini.com/de-de/insights/research/how-sustainability-is-fundamentally-changing-consumer-preferences/

Case, A. (2015). *Calm Technology: Principles and Patterns for Non-Intrusive Design.* Gravenstein Highway North: O'Reilly Media.

ConPolicy. (2020). *Leitfaden zur Erarbeitung von Nudges.* Retrieved June 2025, from https://green-nudging.de/wp-content/uploads/2020/06/Green-Nudging_Leitfaden.pdf

Council of Europe. (2024). Retrieved June 2025, from Guidelines for the use of language as a driver of inclusivity.: https://rm.coe.int/guidelines-for-the-use-of-language-as-a-driver-of-inclusivity/1680aec235

Crawford, C., & Joler, V. (2018). *Anatomy of an AI System.* Retrieved June 2025, from https://anatomyof.ai/

Deloitte. (2024). *Center for Technology Media & Telecommunications.* Retrieved July 2025, from As generative AI asks for more power, data centers seek more reliable, cleaner energy solutions.: https://www2.deloitte.com/us/en/insights/industry/technology/technology-media-and-telecom-predictions/2025/genai-power-consumption-creates-need-for-more-sustainable-data-centers.html?utm_source=chatgpt.com

Deloitte Global. (n.d.). *Deloitte CxO Sustainability Reports.* Retrieved June 2025, from https://www.deloitte.com

Deutsches Institut für Normung. (2011). *Ergonomie der Mensch-System-Interaktion - Teil 210: Prozess zur Gestaltung gebrauchstauglicher interaktiver Systeme (ISO 9241-210:2010); Deutsche Fassung EN ISO 9241-210:2010.* Berlin: Beuth Verlag GmbH.

Deutsches Institut für Normung. (2018). *DIN EN ISO 9241 Teil 11. Gebrauchstauglichkeit: Begriffe und Konzepte.* Berlin: Beuth Verlag GmbH.

Deutsches Institut für Normung. (2020). *Ergonomie der Mensch-System-Interaktion - Teil 210: Menschzentrierte Gestaltung interaktiver Systeme (ISO 9241-210:2019); Deutsche Fassung EN ISO 9241-210:2019.* Berlin: Beuth Verlag GmbH.

Deutsches Institut für Normung. (2023). *E DIN SPEC 33429:2023-04 "Empfehlungen für Deutsche Leichte Sprache".* Berlin: Beuth Verlag.

Deutsches Institut für Normung. (2024). *DIN 8581-1:2024-05 Einfache Sprache - Anwendung für das Deutsche - Teil 1: Sprachspezifische Festlegungen.* Berlin: Beuth Verlag.

Dobres, J., Chahine, N., & Reimer, B. (2017). Effects of ambient illumination, contrast polarity, and letter size on text legibility under glance-like reading. *Applied Ergonomics*(Volume 60), pp. 68-73. Retrieved from https://doi.org/10.1016/j.apergo.2016.11.001.

Dornauer, B., & Felderer, M. (2023). *Web Image Formats: Assessment of Their Real-World-Usage and Performance across Popular Web Browsers.* Retrieved from https://arxiv.org/pdf/2310.00788

Dr. Rohleder, B. (2024). *Bitkom e.V.* Retrieved from Rechenzentren in Deutschland: https://www.bitkom.org/sites/main/files/2024-11/241121-PK-Bitkom-Charts-Rechenzentren-2024-final.pdf

Ecker, M. (2015). *Usability und Usability Engineering zur Gestaltung von Lernsystemen. User-centered Methoden zur nachhaltigen Entwicklung digitaler Bildungsangebote.* Weingarten: Pädagogische Hochschule Weingarten.

Ecklington, J. (1998). *Cannibals with Forks: The Triple Bottom Line of 21st Century Business.* New Society Publishers.

Efoui-Hess, M. (2019). *Climate Crisis: The unsustainable use of online Video.* The Shift Project.

EnChroma. (2021). *Study finds overwhelming evidence that color blindness hinders learning in school.* Retrieved June 2025, from https://enchroma.com/pages/study-finds-overwhelming-evidence-that-color-blindness-hinders-learning-in-school

Erlach, B., Fuss, S., Geden, O., Glotzbach, U., Henning, H.-M., Pittel, K., ... Strefler, J. (2022). *Was sind negative Emissionen, und warum brauchen wir sie? (Kurz erklärt!).* Retrieved June 2025, from Akademienprojekt „Energiesysteme der Zukunft" (ESYS): https://www.leopoldina.org/fileadmin/redaktion/Publikationen/Nationale_Empfehlungen/2022_ESYS_KurzErklärt_Neg.Emissionen.pdf

Europäische Investitionsbank. (2023). Retrieved June 2025, from 81 Prozent der jungen Deutschen achten bei der Jobwahl auf die Haltung des Arbeitgebers zum Klima.: https://www.eib.org/de/press/all/2023-123-81-of-young-germans-say-the-climate-impact-of-prospective-employers-is-an-important-factor-when-job-hunting

European Institute for Gender Equality. (2024). Retrieved June 2025, from Words matter: Supporting gender equality through language and communication.: https://eige.europa.eu/newsroom/news/your-words-matter-new-guide-gender-inclusive-language-and-communication

European Parliament & Council of the European Union. (2024). (Official Journal of the European Union) Retrieved June 2025, from Regulation (EU) 2024/1689 of the European Parliament and of the Council of 13 June 2024 laying down harmonised rules on artificial intelligence (Artificial Intelligence Act).: https://artificialintelligenceact.eu/the-act/

Eyal, N. (2014). *Hooked. How to Build Habit-Forming Products.* New york: Portfolio/Penguin.

Fernández, M., Casanova, E., & Alonso, I. (2015). *Review of Display Technologies Focusing on Power Consumption.* Retrieved June 2025, from https://doi.org/10.3390/su70810854

Fink, F., & Moeller, M. (2022). *Playbook Purpose Driven Organisations. Der Navigator für Purpose Driven in Ihrem Unternehmen.* Stuttgart: Schäfer-Poeschel Verlag.

Fogg, B. (2020). *Tiny Habits. The Small Changes That Change Everything.* New York: HarperCollins.

Frick, T. (2016). *Designing for Sustainability: A Guide to Building Greener Digital Products and Services.* Gravenstein Highway North: O'Relly.

Global Carbon Project. (2023). *CO_2-Emissionen: Größte Länder nach Anteil am weltweiten CO_2-Ausstoß im Jahr 2022.* (Statista) Retrieved June 2025, from https://de.statista.com/statistik/daten/studie/179260/umfrage/die-zehn-groessten-co2-emittenten-weltweit/

Global Sustainable Turism Council. (2024). *GTSC MICE Criteria.* Retrieved June 2025, from https://www.gstcouncil.org/wp-content/uploads/GSTC-MICE-Criteria-2024-2.pdf

Google Search Central. (2010). *Google Search Central.* Retrieved June 2025, from https://developers.google.com/search/blog/2010/04/using-site-speed-in-web-search-ranking?hl=de

Google Search Central. (2018). *Google Search Central.* Retrieved June 2025, from https://developers.google.com/search/blog/2018/01/using-page-speed-in-mobile-search?hl=de

Google Search Zentral. (2024). *Best Practices für mobile Websites und die Mobile-First-Indexierung.* Retrieved June 2025, from https://developers.google.com/search/docs/crawling-indexing/mobile/mobile-sites-mobile-first-indexing?hl=de

Gröger, J., Liu, R., Stobbe, D. L., Druschke, J., & Richter, N. (2021). *Green Cloud Computing. Lebenszyklusbasierte Datenerhebung zu Umweltwirkungen des Cloud Computing.* Retrieved from https://www.umweltbundesamt.de/sites/default/files/medien/5750/publikationen/2021-06-17_texte_94-2021_green-cloud-computing.pdf

Greenwood, T. (2019). *20 ways to make your website more energy efficient.* (Wholegrain Digital) Retrieved from https://www.wholegraindigital.com/blog/website-energy-efficiency/

Greenwood, T. (2019). *Wholegrain Digital.* Retrieved from 20 ways to make your website more energy efficient: https://www.wholegraindigital.com/blog/website-energy-efficiency/

Harley, A. (2019). *Touch Targets on Touchscreens.* Retrieved June 2025, from https://www.nngroup.com/articles/touch-target-size/

Hartson, R. P. (2019). *The UX Book. Agile UX Design for a Quality User Experience.* Amsterdam: Morgan Kaufmann.

Hazas, M. (2023). *The IT sector has a problematic growth rate.* (U. Universitat, Ed.) Retrieved June 2025, from https://www.uu.se/en/news/2023/2023-03-07-the-it-sector-has-a-problematic-growth-rate

Hintemann, R. (2017). *Borderstep.* Retrieved June 2025, from Boom führt zu deutlich steigendem Energiebedarf der Rechenzentren in Deutschland im Jahr 2017.: https://www.borderstep.de/wp-content/uploads/2018/12/Borderstep-Rechenzentren-2017-final-Stand-Dez_2018n.pdf

Hintemann, R., & Hinterholzer, S. (2020). *Borderstep.* Retrieved June 2025, from Videostreaming: Energiebedarf und CO2-Emissionen. Hintergrundpapier: https://www.borderstep.de/publikation/hintemann-r-hinterholzer-s-2020-videostreaming-energiebedarf-und-co2-emissionen-hintergrundpapier-berlin-borderstep-institut/

Hospers, G.-J., & Amrhein, S. (2023). Slowbalisation oder Slowwashing? Eine Analyse des Cittaslow-Konzepts als Strategie für eine wachstumsunabhängige Stadtentwicklung. *RaumPlanung 222*, pp. 21-25.

Inclusion Europe. (2017). Retrieved 2025 June, from Informationen für alle Europäische Regeln, wie man Informationen leicht lesbar und leicht verständlich macht.: https://www.inclusion-europe.eu/wp-content/uploads/2017/06/DE_Information_for_all.pdf

Indrejak, S. (2024). *Kulturwandel im Unternehmen. Praktische Tipps für eine erfolgreiche interne Transformationsbegleitung.* Freiburg, München, Stuttgart: Haufe Group.

Interessenverband der Farbsehschwachen und Farbenblinden e.V. (2024). *Farbsehschwächen & Farbenblindheit.* Retrieved June 2025, from https://www.farbsehschwaeche.de/themen/farbsehschwaechen-und-farbenblindheit-allgemein

International Plain Language Federation. (2025). Retrieved June 2025, from Document design pattern library: https://www.iplfederation.org/wp-content/uploads/2025/06/ISOpatternlibrary06.pdf

IPCC. (1992). *Climate Change: The 1990 and 1992 IPCC Assessments.* Retrieved June 2025, from https://www.ipcc.ch/site/assets/uploads/2018/05/ipcc_90_92_assessments_far_full_report.pdf

IPCC. (2019). Zusammenfassung für politische Entscheidungsträger. *IPCC-Sonderbericht über den Ozean und die Kryosphäre in einem sich wandelnden Klima.* (H.-O. Pörtner, D. Roberts, V. Masson-Delmotte, P. Zhai, M. Tignor, E. Poloczanska, . . . N. Weyer, Eds., & C. Best, Trans.) Bonn.

IPCC. (2023). *Summary for Policymakers. In: Climate Change 2023: Synthesis Report. Contribution of Working Groups I, II and III to the Sixth Assessment Report of the Intergovernmental Panel on Climate Change.* Retrieved June 2025, from IPCC: https://www.ipcc.ch/report/ar6/syr/downloads/report/IPCC_AR6_SYR_SPM.pdf

Islam, M. R., Hurwitz, D. S., & Wyman, A. A. (2017). *Safer driver responses at intersections with green signal countdown timers, Transportation Research Part F: Traffic Psychology and Behaviour, Volume 51, 2017, Pages 1-13, ISSN 1369-8478*. Retrieved from https://doi.org/10.1016/j.trf.2017.08.010

ISO - International Organisation for Standardization. (2018). *ISO 9241-11:2018(en) Ergonomics of human-system interaction - Part 11: Usability: Definitions and concepts.* Retrieved June 2025, from https://www.iso.org/standard/63500.html

ISO - International Organisation for Standardization. (2023). Retrieved June 2025, from ISO 24495-1:2023, Plain language Part 1: Governing principles and guidelines: https://www.iso.org/standard/78907.html

Istrate, R., Tulus, V., Grass, R. N., Vanbever, L., Stark, V. J., & Guillén-Gosálbez, G. (2024). *The environmental sustainability of digital content consumption.* Retrieved from https://doi.org/10.1038/s41467-024-47621-w

IUCN. (1980). *World Conservation Strategy: Living Resource Conservation for Sustainable Development. IUCN.* Retrieved June 2025, from https://portals.iucn.org/library/efiles/documents/wcs-004.pdf

Johnson, S. (2023). *Companies with good ESG scores pollute as much as low-rated rivals.* Retrieved from Financial Times: https://www.ft.com/content/b9582d62-cc6f-4b76-b0f9-5b37cf15dce4

Kahnemann, D. (2011). *Thinking Fast and Slow.* New York: Farrar, Straus and Giroux.

Karaosman, H., Brun, A., & Morales-Alonso, G. (2016). Handbook of Research on Global Fashion Management and Merchandising. (A. Vecchi, & C. Buckley, Eds.) *Slow Fashion and Sustainability: The Luxury Impact.*

Kauer-Franz, M. F. (2022). *Usability und User Experience Design: Das umfassende Handbuch.* Rheinwerk Verlag.

Kaya, R. T., & Murano, P. (2022). *Is carousel interaction really usable?* (First Monday) Retrieved June 2025, from https://firstmonday.org/ojs/index.php/fm/article/view/11801/11155

KPMG. (2021). *Customer Experience Excellence Studie 2021.* (KPMG Customer Insights Hub) Retrieved June 2025, from https://hub.kpmg.de/customer-experience-excellence-studie-2021

Krug, S. (2014). *Don't Make Me Think. Web & Mobile usability - Das intuitive Web.* mitp Verlags GmbH & Co KG.

Laker, B. (2023). *Greenwashing Unmasked: A Critical Examination Of ESG Ratings And Actual Environmental Footprint.* Retrieved from Forbes: https://www.forbes.com/sites/benjaminlaker/2023/08/04/navigating-the-mirage-unraveling-the-disconnect-between-esg-ratings-and-real-environmental-impact/

Lambrecht, U., Kräck, J., & Dünnebeil, F. (2021). *Homeoffice und Ersatz von Dienst- und Geschäftsreisen durch Videokonferenzen. Potenziale zur Minderung der Treibhausgasemissionen unter Berücksichtigung der Erfahrungen aus der Corona-Krise.* Retrieved June 2025, from ifeu paper 04/2021: https://www.ifeu.de/fileadmin/uploads/IFEU-Workingpaper_4-_21_-__Mobiles_Arbeiten_und_Videokonferenzen.pdf

Lamont, D. (2022). *Sind nachhaltigere Unternehmen höher bewertet?* Retrieved June 2025, from Schroders plc.: https://www.schroders.com/de-de/de/privatanleger/insights/sind-nachhaltigere-unternehmen-hoher-bewertet/

Liebe, U., Gewinner, J., & Diekmann, A. (2021). *Large and persistent effects of green energy defaults in the household and business sectors.* Retrieved June 2025, from Nature Human Behaviour: https://www.researchgate.net/publication/349993275_Large_and_pe

rsistent_effects_of_green_energy_defaults_in_the_household_and_business_sectors

Little, A. (2004). *An interview with Patagonia founder Yvon Chouinard.* Retrieved June 2025, from https://grist.org/technology/little-chouinard/

Lutz, D. (2022). *The Life-centered Design Guide.*

Lutz, D. (2023). *The Non-Human Persona Guide.* Damien Lutz.

Lyle, J. T. (1996). *Regenerative design for sustainable development.* John Wiley & Sons Inc.

Marks, L. (2022). *Ask an Environmental Expert: What's the Carbon Footprint of the Internet?* Retrieved June 2025, from https://thewalrus.ca/carbon-footprint-internet/

Meadows, D. H., Meadows, D. L., Randers, J., & Behrens, W. W. (1972). *Limits to Growth. A Report for the Club of Rome's Project on the Predicament of Mankind.* New York: Universe Books.

Microsoft. (2024). *Nachhaltigkeit.* Retrieved June 2025, from https://www.microsoft.com/de-de/berlin/nachhaltigkeit.aspx

Minjeong, K., & Hoe, K. K. (2020). *Investigation of environmental benefits of traffic signal countdown timers, Transportation Research Part D: Transport and Environment, Volume 85, 2020, 102464, ISSN 1361-9209.* Retrieved June 2025, from https://doi.org/10.1016/j.trd.2020.102464

Molzbichler, K. (2019). *Nachhaltiges Design und User Experience. Digitale Transformation und die Auswirkungen der Gestaltung auf Mensch und Umwelt.* München: Oekom.

Nielsen, J. (2012). *Usability 101: Introduction to Usability.* Retrieved from Nielsen Norman Group: https://www.nngroup.com/articles/usability-101-introduction-to-usability/

Nomura, M. S. (2010). *International Federation of Library Association and Institutions.* Retrieved June 2025, from Guidelines for easy-to-read materials: https://www.ifla.org/wp-content/uploads/2019/05/assets/hq/publications/professional-report/120.pdf

Norman, D. (2013). *The Design of Everyday Things: Revised and Expanded Edition.* Basic Books.

Norman, D. (2023). *Design for a better World: Meaningful, sustainable, humanity centered.* Cambridge, Messachusetts: MIT Press.

Norman, D. A. (2004). *Emotional Design: Why We Love (or Hate) Everyday Thinks.* New York: Basic.

OECD. (2025). Retrieved June 2025, from Behind ESG Ratings. Unpacking sustainability metrics.: https://www.oecd.org/content/dam/oecd/en/publications/reports/2025/02/behind-esg-ratings_4591b8bb/3f055f0c-en.pdf

Ognen, R., Thomson, T., & Scores, R. E. (2018). Retrieved June 2025, from Thomson Reuters ESG Scores: https://www.esade.edu/itemsweb/biblioteca/bbdd/inbbdd/archivos/Thomson_Reuters_ESG_Scores.pdf

Okabe, M., & Ito, K. (2008). Retrieved June 2025, from Color Universal Design (CUD) - How to make figures and presentations that are friendly to Colorblind people: https://jfly.uni-koeln.de/color/#:~:text=Use%20not%20only%20different%20colors,cannot%20distinguish%20differences%20in%20color.&text=Clearly%20state%20color%20names%20where,use%20color%20names%20in%20communication.

OVO Energy. (2019). *'Think Before You Thank': If every Brit sent one less thank you email a day, we would save 16,433 tonnes of carbon a year – the same as 81,152 flights to Madrid*. Retrieved from https://company.ovo.com/think-before-you-thank-if-every-brit-sent-one-less-thank-you-email-a-day-we-would-save-16433-tonnes-of-carbon-a-year-the-same-as-81152-flights-to-madrid/

Peppers, D., & Rogers, M. (1993). *The One to One Future: Building Relationships One Customer at a Time.* Currency Doubleday.

Pernice, K. (n.d.). *Designing Effective Carousels for Websites and Mobile Apps.* (Nielsen Norman Group) Retrieved June 2025, from https://www.nngroup.com/videos/carousels-websites-mobile-apps/

Persson, H., Åhman, H., Yngling, A., & Gulliksen, J. (2014). Universal Access in the Information Society. In C. Stephanidis, *Universal design, inclusive design, accessible design, design for all: different concepts—one goal? On the concept of accessibility—historical, methodological and philosophical aspects* (Vol. 14, pp. 505–526). Retrieved from Universal design, inclusive design, accessible design, design for all: different concepts—one goal? On the concept of accessibility—historical, methodological and philosophical aspects.: https://doi.org/10.1007/s10209-014-0358-z

Piepenbrock, C., Mayr, S., Mund, I., & Buchner, A. (2013). Positive display polarity is advantageous for both younger and older adults. *ergonomics*(56 (7)), pp. 1116–1124. Retrieved from https://doi.org/10.1080/00140139.2013.790485

Plain Language Association International. (2025). *Plain Language Association International.* Retrieved June 2025, from https://plainlanguagenetwork.org

Pratt, A., & Nunes, J. (2012). *Interactive Design. An Introduction to the Theory and Application of User-Centered Design.* Rockport Publishers.

Quack, D., & Oley, M. (2002). Environmental Advantages of Video Conferencing Systems – Results from a Simplified LCA. *Environmental Communication in the Information Society - Proceedings of the 16th Conference*, pp. 446-450. Retrieved from Environmental Communication in the Information Society - Proceedings of the 16th Conference.

Radicati Group. (2024). *Prognose zur Anzahl der täglich versendeten und empfangenen E-Mails weltweit von 2021 bis 2026.* (Statista) Retrieved June 2025, from https://de.statista.com/statistik/daten/studie/252278/umfrage/prognose-zur-zahl-der-taeglich-versendeter-e-mails-weltweit/

Ramirez, B. L. (2020). *Green by Default. This simple psychological trick could vastly reduce tech's carbon footprint.* Retrieved June 2025, from https://screenspan.net/blog/green-by-default/

Rams, D. (2017). *Zehn Thesen für gutes Design.* Prestel.

Roland, E. (2021). *Eight Forms of Capital.* Retrieved June 2025, from Permaculture: http://appleseedpermaculture.com/wp-content/uploads/2011/04/8_Forms_of_Capital_PM68.pdf

Roland, E., & Landua, G. (2013). *Regenerative Enterprise: Optimizing for Multi-Capital Abundance.* Lulu.com.

Saenko, K. (2024). *Scientific American.* Retrieved June 2025, from A Computer Scientist Breaks Down Generative AI's Hefty Carbon Footprint.: https://www.scientificamerican.com/article/a-computer-scientist-breaks-down-generative-ais-hefty-carbon-footprint/

Sanford, C. (2017). *The Regenerative Business: Redesign Work, Cultivate Human Potential, Achieve Extraordinary Outcomes* (2. Aufl. ed.). Boston: Nicholas Brealey Publishing.

Santos, O., Ribeiro, F., Metrôlho, J., & Dionísio, R. (2024). *Using Smart Traffic Lights to Reduce CO2 Emissions and Improve Traffic Flow at Intersections: Simulation of an Intersection in a Small Portuguese City.* Retrieved June 2025, from https://doi.org/10.3390/asi7010003

Scharinger, C., Kammerer, Y., & Gerjets, P. (2016). *Kognitive Belastungen beim Lesen im Internet: Was Pupillengröße und Hirnströme verraten können.*

Retrieved June 2025, from https://www.innovations-report.de/fachgebiete/kommunikation-medien/kognitive-belastungen-beim-lesen-im-internet-was-pupillengroesse-und-hirnstroeme-verraten-koennen/

Schumacher, R. (2009). *The handbook of global user research.* San Francisco, Kaliforien: Morgan Kaufmann Publishers Inc.

Senadheera, S., Gregory, R., Rinklebe, J., Farrukh, M., Rhee, J., & Ok, Y. S. (2022). Retrieved June 2025, from The development of research on environmental, social, and governance (ESG): A bibliometric analysis. Sustainable Environment.: https://doi.org/10.1080/27658511.2022.2125869

Shedroff, N. (2009). *Design is the Problem. The Future of Design must be Sustainable.* New York: Rosenfeld Media.

Simonetti, L., & Petrini, C. (2012). The ideology of Slow Food. *Journal of European Studies*, pp. 168-189.

Stöveken, S., & Brugger, P. (2018). *Chancenbereich für ökologische und finanzielle Nachhaltigkeit. Wie Unternehmen Nachhaltigkeitspotenziale konsequent nutzen und monetarisieren können.* Retrieved June 2025, from Horváth AG: https://www.horvath-partners.com/de/media-center/white-paper/chancenbereiche-fuer-oekologische-und-finanzielle-nachhaltigkeit

Stanley, A. (2023). *IBD's 100 Best ESG Companies For 2023*. Retrieved June 2025, from Investor's Business Daily: https://www.investors.com/

Statista Research Department. (2024). *Statistiken zum Thema Schwerbehinderung*. Retrieved June 2025, from https://de.statista.com/themen/261/behinderung/

Stumpf, L., & Prof. Dr. Baumgartner, R. J. (2022). *Die Circular Economy – ein Konzept mit vielen Perspektiven.* (A. Böckel, J. Quaing, I. Weissbrod, & J. Böhm, Eds.)

Suhr, F. (2019). *Einmal Plastikmüll to go, bitte*. Retrieved June 2025, from Statista: https://de.statista.com/infografik/18133/verbrauch-von-einwegbechern-in-deutschland/

Sunstein, C. R., & Reisch, R. A. (2018). Greener By Default. *Harvard Law School. The Harvard John M. Olin Discussion Paper Series No. 951*. Retrieved from https://doi.org/10.2139/ssrn.3097488

Suski, P., Pohl, J., & Frick, V. (2020). *Association for Computing Machinery*. Retrieved June 2025, from All you can stream: Investigating the role of user behavior for greenhouse gas intensity of video streaming: https://doi.org/10.1145/3401335.3401709

Sweller, J. (2011). *Psychology of Learning and Motivation* (Vol. 55). Academic Press.

Szyszka, P. (2024). *Storytelling. Eine Geschichte hinter den Geschichten und Narrationen der Kommunikationspraxis.* (P. R. Szyszka, Hrsg.) Wiesbaden: Springer VS.

Thaler, R., & Sunstein, C. (2008). *Nudge. Improving decisions about health, wealth and happiness.* New Heaven & London: Yale University Press.

The Global Compact. (2004). *Who Cares Wins. Connecting the Financial Markets to Changing World?* Retrieved June 2025, from https://www.unglobalcompact.org/docs/issues_doc/Financial_markets/who_cares_who_wins.pdf

The Radicati Group Inc. (2022). *Email Statistics Report, 2022-2026.* Retrieved June 2025, from https://www.radicati.com/?p=17936

The Shift Project. (2019). Retrieved June 2025, from Lean ICT: Towards digital sobriety.: https://theshiftproject.org/wp-content/uploads/2019/03/Lean-ICT-Report_The-Shift-Project_2019.pdf

The Shift Project. (2019). Retrieved June 2025, from Climate Crisis: The unsustainable use of online video.: https://theshiftproject.org/wp-content/uploads/2019/07/2019-02.pdf

Umweltbundesamt. (2023). *Das Energieeffizienzgesetz: Chancen für die Rechenzentrums- und IT-Branche.* Retrieved June 2025, from https://www.umweltbundesamt.de/sites/default/files/medien/11867/dokumente/17052023_policy_paper_enefg_chancen_fuer_die_rechenzentrums_und_it-branche.pdf

UN Climate Change. (2021). *Speech: Mia Mottley, Prime Minister of Barbados at the Opening of the #COP26 World Leaders Summit.* Retrieved June 2025, from https://youtu.be/PN6THYZ4ngM?si=KJ-AKf1rC2JNdU01

UNCED. (1992). *Agenda 21: Konferenz der Vereinten Nationen für Umwelt und Entwicklung.* Retrieved June 2025, from https://www.un.org/depts/german/conf/agenda21/rio.pdf

UNEP Finance Initiative; UN Global Compact. (2006). *Principles for Responsible Investment.* Retrieved June 2025, from https://portal.ct.gov/-/media/ott/pdfs/pri.pdf

Unilever. (2019). Retrieved June 2025, from Unilever Annual Report and Accounts 2018.:

https://www.unilever.com/files/origin/9fbb2cb4402c390d78734e74baa53603223abd8c.pdf/Unilever-Annual-Report-and-Accounts-2018.pdf

United Nations. (1972). Retrieved June 2025, from United Nations Conference on the Human Environment: https://www.un.org/en/conferences/environment/stockholm1972

United Nations. (2000). *United Nations Millenium Summit.* Retrieved June 2025, from https://www.un.org/en/conferences/environment/newyork2000

United Nations. (2006). Retrieved June 2025, from Convention on the Rights of Persons with Disabilities and Optional Protocol.: https://www.un.org/disabilities/documents/convention/convoptprot-e.pdf

United Nations. (2015). *Transforming our world: the 2030 Agenda for Sustainable Development.* Retrieved from https://www.unfpa.org/resources/transforming-our-world-2030-agenda-sustainable-development

Urmersbach, B. (2024). *Statistiken zur Weltbevölkerung. Stand: 2023.* Retrieved June 2025, from Statista: https://de.statista.com/themen/75/weltbevoelkerung/#topicOverview

Verband Deutsches Reisemanagement e.V. (2022). *VDR Gesschäftsreiseanalyse 2022.* Retrieved July 2025, from https://www.vdr-service.de/

Verband Deutsches Reisemanagement e.V. (2023). *8 Schritte zur klimaschonenden Geschäftsreise.* Retrieved July 2025, from https://www.vdr-service.de/

Verband Deutsches Reisemanagement e.V. (2024). *VDR-Geschäftsreiseanalyse 2024.* Retrieved July 2025, from https://www.vdr-service.de/

Verband Deutsches Reisemanagement e.V. (n.d.). *VDR-Geschäftsreiseanalyse 2021.* Retrieved July 2025, from https://www.vdr-service.de/

Vogel, T., & Stahmann, M. (2024). *Drei Regeln zum Farbsehschwäche-gerechten Gestalten.* Retrieved June 2025, from https://www.farbsehschwaeche.de/ratgeber/drei-regeln-farbsehschwaeche-gerecht-gestalten

W3C. (2021). *Web Content Accessibility Guidelines (WCAG) 2.2.* Retrieved June 2025, from World Wide Web Consortium: https://www.w3.org/TR/WCAG22/

W3C. (2024). *Web Sustainability Guidelines 1.0.* Retrieved June 2025, from World Wide Web Consortium: https://w3c.github.io/sustainableweb-wsg/#business-strategy-and-product-management

Walkley, S. (2022). *The Carbon Cost of an Email.* Retrieved June 2025, from Carbon Literacy Project: https://carbonliteracy.com/the-carbon-cost-of-an-email/

Walter, S. (2022). *User Journey Mapping: Visualize User Research, Brainstorm Opportunities, and Solve Problems.* Richmond: SitePoint.

Web Sustainability Guidelines. (2023). *Web Sustainability Guidelines (WSG) 1.0.* Retrieved June 2025, from https://w3c.github.io/sustyweb/

WebAIM. (2021). *Alternative Text.* Retrieved June 2025, from WebAIM. Institute for Disability Research, Policy, and Practice: https://webaim.org/techniques/alttext/

WebAIM. (2025). *The WebAIM Million.* Retrieved June 2025, from The 2025 report on the accessibility of the top 1,000,000 home pages: https://webaim.org/projects/million/?utm_source=chatgpt.com

Weiser, M., & Brown, J. S. (1995). Retrieved June 2025, from Designing Calm Technology.: https://people.csail.mit.edu/rudolph/Teaching/weiser.pdf

WHO. (2023). Retrieved June 2025, from Blindness and vision impairment: https://www.who.int/en/news-room/fact-sheets/detail/blindness-and-visual-impairment

Wright, A. (2022). *Regenerative User Experience. Towards a Heuristics of Post-Capitalist Digital Design Practice.* Retrieved June 2025, from https://alexwright.com/docs/Wright_Dissertation_2022.pdf

WWF. (2021). Retrieved from Aus Wäldern wird Papier: https://www.wwf.de/themen-projekte/waelder/papierverbrauch/zahlen-und-fakten/

Yesilada, Y., & Harper, S. (2019). *Web Accessibility. A Foundation for Research.* London: Springer-Verlag London Ltd.

Zero Waste International Alliance. (2025). Retrieved June 2025, from https://zwia.org/

Zielińska-Szczepkowska, J. (2020). Slow Tourism – The Fashion for Slowness or a Conscious Choice? *Folia Oeconomica Stetinensia 20*, pp. 468-483.

ABOUT THE AUTHOR

Monika Schirmeier is a UX designer based in Germany. With a background in communication design, she brings a human-centered approach to her work—shaped by a strong commitment to sustainability and a deep appreciation for global cultures.

Often working remotely from various locations around the world, Monika draws on her international experiences to inform thoughtful, inclusive digital design. Her focus lies in creating user experiences that are intuitive and accessible, as well as environmentally responsible and resource efficient.

In this publication she shares her vision for a more sustainable approach to UX design—one that considers both user needs and long-term impact. Her goal is to empower others with practical knowledge that supports more thoughtful, responsible design choices.

www.ingramcontent.com/pod-product-compliance
Lightning Source LLC
Chambersburg PA
CBHW050527240926
51846CB00003B/725
* 9 7 8 8 0 1 1 0 6 8 7 9 0 *